Historic Churches
of the
Ottawa Valley

Historic Churches
of the
Ottawa Valley

Alan H. Bentley

GSPH

GENERAL STORE PUBLISHING HOUSE INC.
499 O'Brien Road, Box 415
Renfrew, Ontario, Canada K7V 4A6
Telephone 1.613.432.7697 or 1.800.465.6072
www.gsph.com

ISBN 978-1-77123-008-7

Cover art, design, formatting: Magdalene Carson
Printed by Image Digital Printing Ltd. dba The IDP Group, Renfrew, Ontario
Printed and bound in Canada

Cataloguing data available at Library and Archives Canada

Historic Churches of the Ottawa Valley
is dedicated to my wife, Elizabeth,
and to all of our children and grandchildren.
I hope you enjoy reading it as much
as I have enjoyed putting it together.

Table of Contents

PART TWO: Churches of Fitzroy, Goulbourn, Huntley, Torbolton, and March Townships in Ottawa West

PART THREE: Churches of the Madawaska and Mississippi River Valleys

PART FOUR: Churches of the Rideau Valley

Part Five: Churches of the South-Eastern Ottawa Valley

Acknowledgements

I wish to acknowledge the assistance of my editor, Beverley Humphries, and my graphic designer, Magdalene Carson, of General Store Publishing House, who massaged my words and photographs into a much more acceptable manuscript. Their patience was very much appreciated. A special thank you goes to each of these wonderful and helpful specialists.

Preface

Just after I retired some seventeen years ago, I began a search for books on the churches of Ottawa and its surrounding communities. Such a book did not seem to be readily available, if it existed at all. I wanted to know more about the churches and soon realized that many were built in locations where visitors would not normally see them. I thought that I could bring them into the open with this book.

While doing my research, I quickly realized that there were many more churches than I had envisioned. As of my last count, there are over three hundred churches in the Ottawa area. I therefore decided to include only historical or stone churches that would be of interest to many people. Not only are they beautiful structures, but their numbers could be accommodated between the covers of one book.

Many early settlers came from churches in Europe and brought their religions with them. In the early communities, the churches became a gathering point for the residents and centres of activity. Services were often held in homes. As the community grew and became more established, a small wooden church or a more sturdy stone church was often built to serve the parish's needs. Often churches were lost to fires in the early years, but dedicated parishioners persisted and rebuilt. Many of the churches that we see today have been rebuilt several times. A small number of original churches have survived and remind us of our religious heritage. As we grow older, we develop an interest in where we came from, our ancestors, and the origins of our church families; we are all connected, in one way or another, to a church. This book is not intended to be a complete history of the churches contained between the covers. Rather, it is a snapshot of the early beginnings of many churches in this young country of Canada.

I have personally photographed all the churches contained in this book. These photographs are of the exterior; the interiors are for you to explore at your leisure. The many artefacts contained in the structures and the beauty of the stained glass windows will make any visit worthwhile.

The writing of this book has taken longer than it should have, but thanks to the urgings of my loving wife and partner, it has been completed for you to enjoy. I thank her for her editing skills and her patience, as there were times when she did not think the book would come to fruition.

Alan H. Bentley

PART ONE

Churches of Ottawa
within View of
the Parliament Buildings

All Saints Anglican Church, Sandy Hill

All Saints Anglican is a beautiful church not often seen by visitors to Ottawa. Completed in 1900 and built in the Gothic Revival style, the church has counted many politicians and members of Ottawa's high society among its parishioners, one of the most notable being Prime Minister Sir Robert Borden. The wedding, in 1924, of Lois Frances Booth, granddaughter of lumber baron J.R. Booth, to Prince Erik of Denmark was one of Ottawa's most spectacular weddings. The guest list was a who's who of Ottawa society of that time. To this day, All Saints Anglican Church remains a vibrant church serving the inner-city community of Sandy Hill.

All Saints Anglican Church, Sandy Hill, was the home church of the lumber baron J.R. Booth

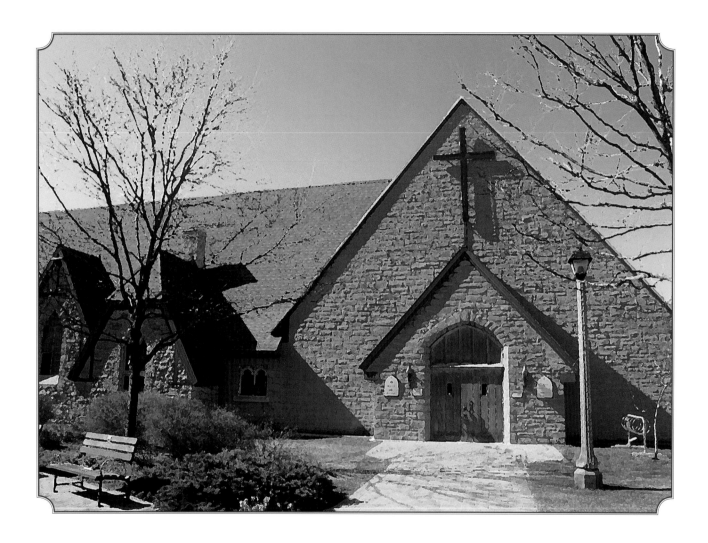

All Saints Anglican Church, Westboro

Construction began on the Chapel of the Holy Spirit, All Saints Anglican, Westboro, in 1865. It has been used for meditation, prayer, and worship ever since.

At that time, Westboro Village was part of Nepean and was located along the banks of the Ottawa River where a number of sawmills once stood. The chapel was built as a church for this community. Marks in the floor were reported to have been made by the hobnails of the lumberjacks. The design, in the Gothic Revival style, was by Thomas Fuller who also designed the Parliament Buildings and other churches in this region. His pictorial rendering of the stone building shows a small belfry in a spire, which does not exist, and a wooden framed entrance porch that is actually built of stone.

The construction took some time, as funds were short. The inner doors of the entrance are finished in grained paintwork, which is believed to be original. The double-diagonal design of the planking of the inner and outer doors and the vestry door forms a pattern reminiscent of the exposed roof joists and the window arches. The outer doors were restored in 1998. The stained-glass windows are relatively new, and dedications and dates can be seen inscribed on them. When visiting the chapel, note the dove and Holy Spirit in the west wall.

All Saints Anglican Church is now serving Anglican and United Church congregations.

Blessed Sacrament Roman Catholic Church, The Glebe

The Blessed Sacrament church community had its beginnings on Easter Tuesday, March 25, 1913. The parish had inherited, as a dowry, land from St. Patrick's parish, so a church had to be built. On May 8, 1932, the new church was blessed and opened for worship. In his "A History of Blessed Sacrament," found on the church's website, John Grace states the following, "The completion and opening of the new building is the most exciting event in the history of 'The Blessed Sacrament Church' to give the full title which its founding pastor preferred."

The first thing that could be said about the church is that in its time it was quite unlike any other Catholic church in Ottawa and probably the country. Elegant and uncluttered, the interior might seem bare without the colour and decoration, which parishioners associated with a Roman Catholic church in that period. This new structure looked more Protestant than Catholic, and the apparent severity caused a stir. To understand the impact, one should compare this church to other Catholic churches of the time with which people were familiar: St. Patrick's, the mother church; St. Brigid's; or the old St. Joseph's Church (all three of the churches can be found on other pages of this book).

John Grace indicates that "one of the interesting things about the church is its different appearance at different times of the day and in different seasons of the year. In bright sunlight its various shades of light Indiana limestone shine with splendour; in moonlight its outlines have an enchanting appearance; lighted at night its traceried windows pour out light and the rose window reveals to the outside world its seven archangels; but perhaps the church is most beautiful when covered with a mantle of snow."

Angus L. MacDonald, the former premier of Nova Scotia and a member of the War Cabinet (for the Navy) lived in the parish during the 1939 to 1945 war years, and his tall, distinguished figure became quickly familiar at Sunday mass.

The stained glass windows on both sides of the nave cost $20,000. When they were first seen publicly, circa May 1953, the windows were described by the Ottawa Journal of that time as "outstanding examples of the glaziers' art." The windows are the work of world-famous sculptors from Munich, Germany, and rate among the most beautiful in North America and beyond. It took eighteen months to complete the windows and two days to install them.

Blessed Sacrament Roman Catholic Church is both elegant and uncluttered.

Christ Church Cathedral, Centretown West

Ottawa was an unremarkable place when it was born in 1826 as Bytown, a Rideau Canal construction camp. At that time, life at the confluence of the Rideau, Gatineau, and Ottawa rivers was focused on Wrightsville, now Gatineau, which was founded in 1800. It was there that the first Anglican church in the region, St. James, opened in 1824.

In that same year, Nicholas Sparks paddled across the Ottawa River to carve a homestead out of the woods on the south side. Just two years later, Colonel John By and his engineers arrived to start the canal. Once the canal began turning the shantytown into a centre of commerce, Bytown Anglicans wanted a church of their own.

According to the Christ Church website, plans were made in April 1832 to build "an Episcopal Church in Bytown," 50 feet by 30 feet, on a site donated by Nicholas Sparks. Just over a year later, Richard Thomas had built a stone Regency Gothic Revival house of worship.

It was originally a plain little building; however, in 1841, transepts, a chancel, a tower, and a tin roof were added to the church. Bytown was booming by now, and in 1855 the church had to build galleries supported by iron columns to hold its growing congregation.

Bishop John Lewis's plans, beginning as early as 1871, to divide the Diocese of Ontario — which would require a cathedral — led Christ Church to build anew. Thomas W. Fuller was asked to design a church "harmonizing with the improvements taking place in the architecture of the city [reference to the Parliament Buildings]," as noted once again in the church's website.

The resulting design by architect King Arnoldi was a full-blown, individualistic Victorian Gothic Revival composition, although it was built with a chancel just one quarter the size proposed. The step-gables at the front and back, ball-flowers (symbolizing the Trinity) in the cornice below the daring broach spire, and the elaborate vine hinges of the front doors made for a strong picturesque exterior. The steep sloping sill of the west window was copied from Parliament Hill's East Block. Inside, slender marble columns, bearing the massive weight of the clerestory walls copied from the House of Commons, revealed daring engineering. They lead the eye up to finely carved flowers and foliage on the stone capitals — a visual pun appropriate to a young capital emerging out of the wilderness. Overhead, the ceiling features a forest of open timbers. Challenged for size in 1932, the congregation built a larger chancel containing the chapel, organ transept, and sacristy, which was designed in academic Gothic style by A.J. Hazelgrove.

Christ Church Cathedral viewed from the back, showing the sanctuary.

Church of St. Matthias Anglican, Civic Hospital

St. Matthias Anglican parish has lived in two different church buildings since it was founded in 1888. The first was built in 1890 on Fairmont Avenue, and in 1921 a parish hall was added. At that time, there were no houses south of the railway line (now the Queensway) and none northwest of Holland Avenue and Wellington Street. In 1936, a venture was started to look at abandoning the first church in favour of building a new church to accommodate an expanding congregation. The current site of St. Matthias was chosen in 1937 at the southeast corner of Parkdale and the CNR tracks (now the Queensway). The challenge was great, for at the end of 1937 the bank balance was fifty dollars. The land was purchased and paid for by June 24, 1938. The sod turning took place on June 1, 1939, and the first service of dedication took place November 5, 1939.

Along came the Second World War, however, and services continued to be held in the basement of the new church for the next ten years. Following the war, the plans called for a completely finished church in limestone, with cut stone facings, but the cost became prohibitive. In 1947, it was recommended that the north, south, and east walls be constructed of cinder block, with the windows and doorways faced with cut stone. The west front would be constructed of solid Nepean limestone in accordance with the original plans. By 1947, the present design, based on the Early English Gothic style, was approved. On Sunday, May 29, 1949, the first service was held upstairs, and although only centre-aisle pews were installed, a total of 696 parishioners attended the 11:00 a.m. service. The church was formally dedicated on November 2, 1949.

St. Matthias stands today at the corner of the Queensway and Parkdale Avenue as a beautiful stone memorial to the dedicated parishioners, who remained loyal to it throughout many difficult years. As stated in the parish history, written to mark the church's centennial in 1988: "a church building is different from all other buildings, without exception. It is a fountainhead of devotion to God from which springs an awareness of the needs of others, an awareness of what God wants his people to do in this world, and the determination to spend and be spent in Christian service."

St. Matthias Anglican, a church different from all other buildings.

Dominion Chalmers United Church, Centretown

The structure that was to eventually become Chalmers United Church was built in the period from 1912 to 1913 by Bank Street Presbyterian Church, established in 1865. In 1877, the large Dominion Methodist Church (later Dominion United) was built at the corner of Queen and Metcalfe streets. Unfortunately, the building was lost in a fire in 1961.

In 1962, Dominion United and Chalmers United congregations amalgamated under the new name Dominion Chalmers United Church at the Chalmers site. The present church building is a combination of Romanesque architecture on the outside and Byzantine architecture in the 1,000-seat sanctuary. Renovations begun in 2002 and completed in 2004 restored the sanctuary to its original form, reopening the dome. The magnificent four-manual Casavant pipe organ provides wonderful music for church services, as well as for other events. In 2012, Dominion Chalmers celebrated the one hundredth anniversary of the laying of the cornerstone of the original Presbyterian church, which became Chalmers United Church, and the fiftieth anniversary of the amalgamation of Dominion and Chalmers.

Dominion Chalmers United Church, a frequent site of concerts and recitals.

Église Unie St-Marc, Centretown

Founded in 1874, the original Presbyterian church was situated on Wellington Street. In 1965, the church moved to its present location on the corner of Lewis and Elgin streets. Originally serving the Francophone community, the church now serves a cosmopolitan community. The church became a mission of the United Church of Canada in 1925; it will celebrate its 137th year serving the community of Ottawa in 2012.

Eglise Unie St-Marc serves a cosmopolitan community in Ottawa.

Erskine Presbyterian Church, Centretown

The congregation of Erskine Presbyterian Church was established in 1874. The first church was built in 1877 and the second in 1887. The latter was destroyed in the Great Fire of 1900. A new church was purchased, and the current church was built in 1906. During the time of church union that resulted in the formation of the United Church of Canada in 1925, this congregation remained with the Presbyterian Church. Erskine Presbyterian Church was sold in June 2009 and is now the home of the Peace Tower Church, which is affiliated with the Pentecostal Assemblies of Canada. The church building remains one of the beautiful stone churches of Ottawa and is located on Bronson Avenue.

Erskine Presbyterian Church has been affected by the changing times.

First Baptist Church, Downtown

The congregation of First Baptist Church was established in 1857. The present church edifice was designed by architect James Mather in the Gothic Revival style. Construction began in the spring of 1877. The cornerstone of the current church was laid by the Right Honourable Alexander Mackenzie, then prime minister of Canada, who worshipped at First Baptist Church while in Ottawa. The Prime Minister, himself an expert stonemason, disdained the ceremonial trowel offered to him and, borrowing a workman's implement, took off his coat, spread the mortar, set the stone, tapped it in place with the heavy tool, and, as recorded in the church's website, declared it to be "well and truly laid." The ceremonial trowel, donated to the church by the Mackenzie family, can be seen on the north wall of the sanctuary. The first service in the current sanctuary of First Baptist Church at the corner of Laurier Avenue and Elgin Street was held on September 29, 1878.

The original church families of First Baptist had an important influence on the development of Ottawa and their church. To learn more about the importance of the church families and their contributions to Ottawa's rich history, visit the First Baptist Church website. Your interest will become contagious as you read about the lumber barons, 24 Sussex Drive (the Prime Minister's residence), and many interesting families.

First Baptist Church also serves as a garrison church (church home) for members of the Armed Forces posted outside of Ottawa.

First Baptist Church represents the Gothic Revival Style of architecture.

First United Church, Centretown

This church is the former home of the First United Church at the corner of Kent and Florence streets. One of Ottawa's oldest congregations, the church community formed in 1846. In the middle of the nineteenth century, the church was the site of the first mixed-race marriage in Canada. Originally Congregationalist, members of that denomination chose to join the United Church when it was formed in 1925. The current building in Centretown was constructed in 1911. In February 1925, it merged with the former Westminster Presbyterian Church congregation (a post-1900 split from Erskine Presbyterian Church), which had voted for the church union that resulted in the formation of the United Church of Canada, and became the First United Church of Ottawa, four months before the official union.

The church began to struggle in the 1970s and 1980s, but in 1987, Reverend Sharon Moon began her seventeen-year tenure at the church and made it a centre of social activism, especially gay rights, fighting poverty, and supporting people with addictions. The church community's support for the diversity of life has drawn many people to the church. In 2007, the congregation sold their historic structure and moved to Westboro where space is shared with an Anglican Church of Canada congregation, All Saints, Westboro.

First United Church served one of Ottawa's oldest congregations.

Glebe-St. James United Church, The Glebe

Glebe-St. James United Church is located on part of the 1837 Crown grant of 178 acres from Clergy Reserve lands meant to be "a Glebe to the clergymen of the Church of Scotland," as recorded in the church's website. (Glebe means land set aside in support of the church.) The Glebe trustees of St. Andrew's Presbyterian Church were responsible for these lands. In 1894, the congregation of St. Andrew's authorized a Glebe mission located on Third Avenue. By 1905, the present building, at First Avenue and Lyon Street, was occupied, with St. Andrew's providing the new site and half the cost of construction. J.W.H. Watts was the architect. In 1898, he had designed the first St. Matthew's Anglican Church, an attractive wooden structure, which stood on First Avenue until demolished in 1930. The present Glebe-St. James's organ was installed by the Casavant Brothers in 1929.

Glebe Presbyterian and St. Paul's Methodist congregations joined the United Church of Canada in 1925 at the time of church union. St. Paul's took the name of St. James United to avoid confusion with another St. Paul's United Church in Ottawa.

In 1971, Glebe and St. James became one congregation, choosing the Glebe building as their church home. Various furnishings and memorials from St. James may be found in the present sanctuary.

This church is much admired, and when visiting, one should take note of the beautiful stained glass windows and the wood panelling to be found on the interior below the organ pipes.

Glebe-St. James United Church is located in the heart of the Glebe.

Knox Presbyterian Church, Centretown

K nox church is the second oldest Presbyterian congregation in Ottawa. It has occupied its present location at the corner of Lisgar and Elgin streets since 1932, but its history stretches back more than a century and a half.

In 1844, some parishioners broke away from St. Andrews to start a new congregation. Then in 1865, due to overcrowding, part of the congregation left to form what is today Dominion Chalmers. As the congregation continued to grow, part of the congregation remained behind in what is today St. Paul's-Eastern United Church. Land was acquired for a new church in the prestigious City Hall Square. Opened for worship in 1874, the new stone church was one of the most beautiful places of worship then in the city. This time, the church community made sure that its sanctuary was large enough and had seating for 1,150 people. Prime Minister MacKenzie King's dream for a more beautiful nation's capital led to Knox's relocation to its third and current home. To widen Elgin Street, the 1874 church was expropriated and demolished. The current building was opened in 1932. It is distinguished by a square tower and walls of local Nepean limestone. The stunning interior features tall windows, pointed arches, and colonnades. Stained glass windows were installed in the chancel in 1955; another was installed over the balcony in 1977.

MacKenzie King's dream of a wider Elgin Street resulted in Knox Presbyterian Church's present location.

MacKay United Church, New Edinburgh

Thomas MacKay, a staunch Presbyterian Scotsman and stone mason, came to Ottawa in 1826 to work on the Rideau Canal and built its first eight locks. MacKay bought a thousand acres of land on both sides of the Rideau River, built St. Andrew's Presbyterian Church in 1828, and established the village of New Edinburgh on his property in 1830. In 1838, MacKay moved into Rideau Hall, which would later become the residence of the governor general.

MacKay's grandson William Alexander MacKinnon donated two lots at the corner of MacKay Street and Dufferin Road for a church. The design was drawn up by Robert Surtees: It was to be a building of Gothic architecture made of rubble stone work, 75 by 35 feet, at an estimated cost of $5,000. Completed in 1875, the church was named New Edinburgh Presbyterian. In 1901, the name of the church was changed to MacKay Presbyterian Church. By 1908, the congregation had outgrown the first church and a new church was commissioned. The cornerstone of the present church, designed by H.F. Ballantyne, was laid on May 29, 1909, and in 1925, at the time of church union, the name was again changed to MacKay United Church.

This first church built in 1875 was lighted by three iron chandeliers, each holding six oil lamps. When electricity was installed in 1880, the Ladies Aid paid the bill at a cost of sixty-eight dollars. The iron chandeliers were given away to the Wilson Presbyterian Church in Navan. In the church's centennial year, 1975, one of the iron chandeliers was found in a chicken coop on a Navan farm and returned to MacKay United for restoration and preservation at the church. Its centennial year, 1975, also saw *Highlights from MacKay's History: MacKay United Church, 1875–1975* published. At the 125th anniversary celebration, a distinctive coat of arms, flag, and badge were presented to the church by the Chief Herald of Canada, Robert Douglas Watt.

Thomas MacKay's daughter Cristina donated the manse in 1894. In 1898, individual communion cups were purchased to prevent the spread of disease (diphtheria epidemic). A casual conversation between Thomas Rankin's youngest daughter (then in her nineties) and visitors from the church took place nearly one hundred years later. The original communion vessels were mentioned, and Miss Rankin went to her clothes cupboard, took out the MacKay ewer and goblet, and handed them to the parishioners; they had been in her home for seventy-five years for safekeeping. The visitors returned the artefacts to the church.

Rich in the early history of Ottawa, MacKay United has maintained many of the early relics of this era, and they are on display for all to see.

MacKay United Church is a truly historic church with a modern vision.

Merivale United Church, Ottawa South

The structure that now houses Merivale United Church and its welcoming congregation was built in the period from 1875 to 1876. The church replaced a log meeting house that had served both Anglicans and the Presbyterians since the 1840s. Mr. Arthur Hopper donated the land for the church and the adjacent cemetery. The first minister of Merivale Presbyterian Church was Reverend John L. Gourlay, who served the church from 1851 to 1868. In 1886, he wrote A History of the Ottawa Valley, now a rare book in the main branch of the Ottawa Library. The present Merivale church building was constructed under the pastorate of Reverend Robert Williams, who also served Bells Corners and Westboro. In 1908, Merivale separated from Westboro and continued as a single-point charge. In 1932, Merivale celebrated a centennial dating from its roots as a Presbyterian church in 1832, the year the Rideau Canal was completed.

On May 2, 1976, Merivale United celebrated the one hundredth anniversary of the first service in the present church building. Many came in period costume. The parade was led by Reverend T.C. (Tommy) Douglas riding in a buggy.

Merivale United Church situated on busy Merivale Road.

Notre Dame Cathedral, Lowertown

In 1801, the population of Bytown (now Ottawa) began to grow rapidly. Lumberjacks working in the Outaouais, workers on the Rideau Canal, and American Loyalists arrived steadily. In 1828, local Roman Catholics asked for a church. The first church was built in 1832 but soon became too small. In 1839, Father Cannon received the plans for a new church. It was Father Cannon's intention to build the church of Notre Dame as a stone basilica in the Classical manner then in high favour. In 1841, a building contract for Notre Dame was let, and for three years the handsome ashlar walls of a Classic church grew slowly up to a usable single-storey height at its present Sussex Drive location.

From 1847 on, plans were made to transform the church into a neo-gothic style cathedral. In 1849, Canon Georges Bouillon designed the plans for the interior, based on the Sainte-Chapelle in Paris. In 1858, Bishop Guigues had the satisfaction of seeing the silhouette of the cathedral enhanced by the erection of square bell chambers crowned by soaring, staged, octagonal spires. In 1865, the western facade was completed when the gilded Madonna, a gift of the raftsmen of Ottawa in homage to their special benefactress, was set above the apex of the west gable wall.

Around 1878, Canon Bouillon, the diocesan architect at that time, had a dream of locating his dream church on the Ottawa River and building a larger structure than St. Peter's in Rome. But alas, he was not given the huge sum of $35 million required for the project. Instead, he was allowed to alter Notre Dame behind its Regency Gothic facade and to set Phillippe Parizeau to work carving a rich triforium above the chancel stalls. The interior of Notre Dame became a marvellous kaleidoscope of Victorian texture and colour. The construction was totally completed in 1885.

The oldest church in Ottawa, Notre Dame Cathedral remains one of the most remarkable churches in Canada today. The exterior of the building is not particularly eye-catching, except perhaps for the bell towers. But the elegance of the interior is noteworthy. The sanctuary is sculpted entirely from wood. Many figures from the old and new testaments are represented throughout the cathedral. The central nave with sky-blue ceiling offers a sampling of neo-gothic style from the nineteenth century. The high altar decorated with low reliefs is the work of the famous sculptor, Phillippe Hebert. The stained glass windows draw in patterns of coloured light. The majestic Casavant organ has three keyboards, sixty stops, and four thousand pipes. Notre Dame Cathedral is the product of local architects and craftsmen, who were inspired by their profound faith.

In the 1990s, the cathedral underwent major restorations, which have made it a wonderful place to visit while in Ottawa.

Notre Dame, a neo-Gothic style cathedral, is the oldest church in Ottawa.

Notre-Dame-de-Lourdes-de-Cyrville, Vanier

As early as 1825, French Canadians bought land in the Cyrville area that had been owned by English settlers when the Rideau Canal was built in 1826. The lots had been abandoned because they were located so far from the city. If only they could see those lots now.

Religious beginnings date from 1853, and eventually a parish was established and churches built. However, since it was still considered far from the city, the church struggled to survive. In 1925, the parish was given back to the diocesan clergy but the very next year, the church burned down. A new church was built in 1927 and blessed in 1928. Yet, hardship continued for the community: the wind blew down the bell tower, caterpillars ate the harvest, and drought ruined a full year's hard work. In spite of the odds, the parish survived until dwindling numbers of congregants resulted in the closing of Notre-Dame-de-Lourdes-de-Cyrville in January 2011.

The Notre-Dame-de-Lourdes-de-Cyrville parish goes all the way back to 1825.

Our Lady of the Visitation Roman Catholic Church, South Gloucester

The Church of Our Lady of the Visitation is situated on Lot 28, Concession 4, Rideau Front, in what is now the City of Ottawa. The church predates the establishment of the archdiocese itself. The area on Highway 31, south of the city, was settled largely by Irish immigrants, both Catholic and Protestant. A number of French-speaking families moved to the area in the 1850s. The church's website reports that a small wooden chapel was built around 1830, but when Bishop Guigues visited the area in 1848, he found it to be "such a miserable Chapel, a shaky wooden building, open to the winds and a very sad wooden altar the only piece of furniture in the place."

A new structure, meeting the approval of Bishop Guigues, was begun in 1849. The stone was quarried on the McGee properties. Made of square timber, the pillars were, according to stories told, hauled from the farm of Thomas Daley and his wife, Mary McGee, on the old Prescott Road. This is said to be one of the only churches ever to have been built with a clerestory in which there are no windows. The designer simply enclosed a high-ceilinged nave and lower side aisles with stone and tin—puncturing the flank walls at regular intervals with narrow lancet windows.

The church was completed and formally blessed in July 1852. Bishop Guigues remarked that it was "one of the most beautiful churches of Upper Canada," as noted by the church's website. The interior of the church was finished and the main altar solemnly blessed in August 1861. High above the main entrance of the church in a niche in the facade is a statue of the Virgin Mary. Faded and worn with the mist of time, she stands like a sentinel overlooking all those who enter and leave and all those who have been carried to their last resting place. In 1854, an octagonal steeple was added; in 1980 it was taken down and repaired.

The parish's beautiful stone church of Our Lady of the Visitation with its towering steeple, reaching for the skies, now stands as a monumental memorial to our forefathers.

Our Lady of the Visitation Roman Catholic Church with Our Lady seen in the foreground.

Southminster United Church, Old Ottawa South

Southminster was formed by the amalgamation of Ottawa South Methodist and Calvin Presbyterian to become Southminster United in 1925 and occupies a prominent location at the corner of Aylmer and Bank streets by the Rideau Canal in Ottawa. Southminster looks back on a proud history beginning with the first Methodist and Presbyterian congregations in the area more than 150 years ago, and going back to 1860.

The church building as we know it today was consecrated in 1932 and has served the people of Ottawa through the depression years, the Second World War, the postwar boom, and all succeeding decades. In 1966, a Memorial Centennial Carillon was installed. This beautiful stone church has to be visited to be appreciated. Both its exterior and interior are worthy of visits.

Southminster United Church, sitting on the edge of the Rideau Canal, at Bank Street.

St. Alban the Martyr Anglican Church, Sandy Hill

St. Alban's is the second-oldest Anglican parish, with the oldest Anglican Church building, in Ottawa. The church's website indicates that Thomas Fuller, the senior architect responsible for building the Centre Block of the Parliament Buildings, designed "a most beautiful, well-proportioned church of Early English style" with "transepts, chancel . . . a fine tower and spire" for this congregation. However, the difficult site on a steep side of Sandy Hill made it financially impossible to build to Fuller's plans, so his pupil King Arnoldi was hired to revise them. Arnoldi used as much of Fuller's design as he could but originally omitted the chancel, tower, transepts, and spire; the chancel and transepts were not built until 1877.

St. Alban the Martyr Church represented the height of early Gothic Revival ecclesiastical architecture in the Ottawa region. Unlike previous churches, which were supported by government grants, pew rents, and well-to-do parishioners, this church was completely funded by voluntary contributions, and all seats were free. As the church in which Sir John A. Macdonald and many cabinet ministers worshipped, it set the tone for a style of architecture emulated by the larger churches built in the region for decades to come. Notable architectural features include the low stone walls, lancet arches, bell-cote, and interior stencil work. The interior was seriously rendered in late Victorian transitional style.

St. Alban the Martyr, the oldest Anglican church in Ottawa.

St. Andrew's Presbyterian Church, Downtown

A Presbyterian Church was established in Bytown in 1828 in connection with the Church of Scotland, through the efforts of a number of local businessmen and military officers. Thomas MacKay, a Scottish stonemason, had obtained the contract to build the locks joining the Rideau Canal to the Rideau River. During 1828, there was a lull in construction, and MacKay, not wishing to lose his skilled workmen, put them to work building St. Andrew's Church.

In 1828, a lot was purchased on behalf of the congregation at the corner of Wellington and Kent streets from Nicholas Sparks for £200, and construction began at once. The foundation stone was laid by James Ferguson in April, and by mid-October the building was almost complete. The first service was conducted by Reverend Machar of Kingston, on September 28, 1828.

The church itself was a plain A-frame structure with three windows along each side. There was no steeple or other adorning items on the exterior. The interior was also very plain and seated about 300. The church was reported to be debt free in 1837. By the 1850s, the church building had become too small to accommodate all those who wished to attend services. An addition was constructed in 1855. In 1872, the original structure was completely taken down and the present church built. With the new church came the first pipe organ, built by Samuel Warren of Montreal.

It was during 1925 that the work of preparation and installation of the war memorial window was completed. It was unveiled on Sunday, December 13, 1925, by His Excellency the Right Honourable Lord Byng of Vimy, then governor general of Canada.

Without construction of the Rideau Canal, St. Andrew's probably would not have been built.

Ste-Anne's Roman Catholic Church, Lowertown

Ste-Anne's Parish was founded in 1873 to meet the needs of a growing Francophone population in the community of Ottawa. Ste-Anne's Church was built and blessed in 1874. A traditional Quebec-style church, the building was designed by the architect J.P. Lecourt. The steeply pitched roof and facade sculptures are common to churches of this type.

Ste-Anne's remained a vibrant church for many years, playing a large role in the development of the community and the many organizations it supported. In 1967, in preparation for the one hundredth anniversary of Ste-Anne's, the church was transformed. Everything was restored: the floor, the electricity, the plumbing, the pews, and the interior covering. Stained glass windows, among the most beautiful in Canada, let gently filtered light through to harmonize with the pastel colours used in the décor. The property was designated as a Heritage site in 1978.

In 2010, part of the roof collapsed, and the church had to be temporarily closed. Repairs were made but declining revenues for the maintenance of the church, like so many others, forced the closure of Ste-Anne's in 2011, a truly sad event in the life of the Roman Catholic community of Ottawa! In the spring of 2012, it was announced that the St. Clement Parish would move to a new home at Ste-Anne's, and thus the church would be saved.

Ste-Anne's Roman Catholic Church is a traditional Quebec-style church with a steeply pitched roof.

St. Anthony's Roman Catholic Church, Centretown West

Located in the heart of Ottawa's "Little Italy," St. Anthony's is the home church for many members of Ottawa's Italian community. The church was originally built in 1913, but fires in 1917 and 1929 damaged the church and it had to be reconstructed by many of the very people whom it served. The church is noteworthy for its delicate fresco and polychromatic stained glass windows by Italian artist Guido Nincheri. The same artist was involved with the decoration of the Notre Dame Cathedral, St. Theresa's Church, and St. Patrick's Basilica.

St. Anthony's Roman Catholic Church is the centre of religions life for many in Little Italy.

St. Bartholomew Anglican Church, New Edinburgh

St. Bartholomew Anglican Church is rich in the history of Canada. The list of prime ministers, governors general, and members of royalty who have attended St. Bartholomew's is extensive. The architecture and the interior artefacts that have been preserved are impressive. Located on MacKay Avenue adjacent to the governor general's residence, the church is often attended by members of the household. It was in October 1866, just after the government of the province of Canada had moved to the new capital of Ottawa, and the governor general into Rideau Hall, a meeting was held to organize a mission in the suburban village of New Edinburgh. With the encouragement of the governor general and his wife, Lord and Lady Monck, the parish was formally organized at a meeting on St. Bartholomew's Day, August 14, 1867. On the strength of donations from the governor general, the estate of Thomas MacKay (from which land was bequeathed), and the St. Lawrence Railway — all property holders in the village — an architect, Thomas Seaton Scott of Montreal, was engaged.

The building, which Thomas Seaton Scott designed in 1867, is an admirably simple product of the Gothic Revival of the nineteenth century — when one thinks of the ornament lavished on the larger buildings of the period. Its low buttressed walls of local limestone support a steep roof, which was originally straddled by a belfry over the east end and a little spire over the west; these were removed in 1925, by which time they had deteriorated and funds were lacking for restoration. For a quarter-century, Princess Louise's bells lay on the ground behind the church. On the street side, facing the grounds of Rideau Hall, the roof line is punctuated by iron-created dormers and a small porch. A bronze tablet beside the porch gives civic recognition to the church as a heritage building.

Set into the east wall, facing Victoria Street, is the cornerstone laid by Lord Monck in 1868; it is marked with a bronze tablet. The large east window was originally filled with the "Decorated" Gothic tracery found in the other windows. It acquired its present "Early English" tracery at the time of the installation of the stained glass in 1919. Above the door is the heraldic shield of St. Bartholomew: the three knives of his martyrdom. The shield is both the work and the gift of Mr. Gordon MacPherson of Burlington, Ontario. The history of this church is too extensive to record here. You are encouraged to go to the church's website for the full details. It is a virtual record of royalty's presence in Ottawa.

St. Bartholomew Anglican Church is home to governors general and visiting royalty.

St. Brigid's Roman Catholic Church, Lowertown

St. Brigid's Roman Catholic Church is located on a piece of land not far from the present Notre Dame Basilica on the corner of St. Patrick's and Murray streets in Ottawa. A beautiful church, 150 feet long by 70 feet wide, St. Brigid's was completed and blessed in 1890. It is denoted by its twin steeples of widely varying heights and the beauty of its interior. However, much of the beauty was lost in 1986 when the church was repainted and the original murals were covered over. The murals were restored in 1988 when the church was returned as much as possible to its original state. St. Brigid's importance was recognized when it was declared a historic site by the City of Ottawa in 1980 and again in 1989 when the interior was also given a heritage designation.

Located in the oldest part of Ottawa, St. Brigid's became an inner city parish, and it is here that the Shepherds of Good Hope had their origins. This is one of the most important social agencies in the city. While it has moved from St. Brigid's, the organization remains within the parish. Operating today as an Irish cultural centre, St. Brigid's lives on as a rich and culturally significant part of Ottawa's Irish Catholic history. Having been built largely to serve the Irish community, its current usage is understandable. While St. Brigid's is no longer being used as a church, it is thought of by many people in Ottawa as a church and always will be considered such.

St. Brigid's Roman Catholic Church is now home to the Irish community of Ottawa

St. Charles Roman Catholic Church, Vanier

S t. Charles Parish has another beautiful brick church that has struggled to survive as people have moved to the suburbs from Vanier. The parish was established to support an increase in population that could not be accommodated by Notre-Dames-de-Lourdes-de-Cyrville. In 1908, a new church was built on Beechwood Road. St. Charles closed its doors September 26, 2010, due to the small number of people attending and supporting the church. Hopefully, another congregation will find a use for this beautiful structure.

St. Charles Roman Catholic Church is located in the central Vanier part of Ottawa.

St. Francois d'Assise Roman Catholic Church, Hintonburg

Formed in 1890, the parish of St. Francois d'Assise has been serving members of the Francophone community for 122 years. In 1891, a new church that measured 120 feet long by 48 feet wide was built. The population of the parish grew from the original 130 families and continued to grow even more rapidly after the Hull fire of 1900. By 1914, there were 789 families and the church had become too small. In 1924, the present church was built and was 196 feet long by 120 feet wide in the transepts and 52 feet high from the floor to the top of the vault. There are no columns to crowd the interior. The church was blessed in 1915. It is a beautiful stone church with a grand organ, which was restored in 1988 and is among the most famous organs in Ottawa.

St. Francois d'Assise Roman Catholic Church contains one of the most famous organs in Ottawa.

St. George's Roman Catholic Church, Hintonburg

In 1921, the Roman Catholic community of west Ottawa petitioned for a church. The parish of St. George's was established in 1923. In 1924, an Ottawa architect was engaged. Constructed of brick, St. George's Roman Catholic Church was located on the Piccadilly Avenue street car route, so that church members could easily reach the church.

St. George's Roman Catholic Church was built to serve the people of west Ottawa.

St. Jean Baptiste Roman Catholic Church, Centretown West

The congregation of St. Jean Baptiste goes back to 1872. The first church was built in the period from 1882 to 1883 on a promontory on Primrose Street. In 1900, fire destroyed much of the parish and this was followed by another great fire the following year. In 1930, the church was destroyed by yet another fire. Everything had to be rebuilt. The new stone church, completed in 1931, reminds one of a stone fortress from the Middle Ages, with battlements, a dungeon, and a carillon with forty-seven bells.

St. Jean Baptiste Roman Catholic Church resembles a stone fortress of the Middle Ages.

St. John the Baptist Ukrainian Catholic Shrine, Central Experimental Farm

The sheer beauty of St. John the Baptist Ukrainian Catholic Shrine allows it to be included in this collection of churches in the Ottawa area. From the first year of Ukrainian immigration to Canada in 1891, many Ukrainian immigrants visited Ottawa. Some stopped in the capital on their journey to Western Canada and found temporary employment. The first permanent Ukrainian residents settled in Ottawa in approximately 1905. They worked on the railway, in the lumber industry, in construction, and other manual labour occupations.

In 1908, the Ukrainian community founded the Prosvita (education) Association, the first Ukrainian cultural association in Ottawa. The community's new parish was called the Ruthenian (Latin term for Ukrainians) Catholic Church of St. John the Baptist. The present site on Green Valley Crescent was acquired in 1984. This site is ideally suited for the shrine since it is prominently visible, bordered on the east side by the historic Rideau Canal and on the south by a major thoroughfare, Heron Road. In 1987, the building of the church was completed and designated as a Sobor (Shrine) and a national monument to commemorate the Millennium of Christianity in Ukraine (988–1988).

St. John the Baptist Ukrainian Catholic Shrine, bordering the west side of the Rideau Canal.

St. Joseph's Roman Catholic Church, Sandy Hill

St. Joseph's Parish is an integral part of the history and growth of Ottawa. The parish was founded in 1856, a year after Ottawa was incorporated and a year before Queen Victoria proclaimed the city as the capital. The parish began with seventy parishioners. Over the years, the parish churches have been places of worship for uncounted numbers of parishioners and visitors, including prime ministers, members of Parliament, and Supreme Court justices. They are attracted to St. Joseph's largely by the warmth of its welcome, its openness, and the appeal of its liturgy.

The first church opened in 1857. In the early days, the need for more space led to the opening in 1893 of a new and larger church on the same site. This building lasted until two days after Christmas in 1930 when it was destroyed by fire. A third St. Joseph's church on the site opened in 1932 and it still serves, refurbished and renovated, as the place of worship and meeting centre for the parish.

The site itself has historical roots. It is believed to be the location of the burial ground for labourers killed during the construction from 1826 to 1832 of the Rideau Canal, part of the 200-kilometre waterway linking Ottawa and Kingston. The burial ground was relocated prior to the church construction. A very detailed history of St. Joseph's, *Where the Spirit Lives: A History of St. Joseph's Parish, Ottawa, Ontario, 1856–2006*, was compiled by Terry V. Byrne for the 150th anniversary in 2006.

St. Joseph's Roman Catholic Church today serves the inner city.

St. Mary's Roman Catholic Church, Civic Hospital

Today's St. Mary's Roman Catholic Church rose out of the ashes of a disastrous 1949 fire that destroyed the original church, which had existed since 1891. The rubble was cleaned up by the fall of 1949, and construction started on a new twelfth-century Gothic-style church made from hand-cut Nepean limestone. The new church and altar stone were blessed on June 22, 1951. St. Mary's has been enjoyed by the parishioners ever since. Many of the historical records were lost in the fire of 1949, but today's church, constructed at a cost of $288,000, stands as a testament to the loyal parishioners. The sanctuary is noted for its stained glass windows, executed by the studio of Franz Mayer and Company of Munich, which also worked on the windows of St. Peter's Basilica in Rome. Located on Young Street, the church can be seen as one travels along the Queensway today.

St. Mary's is a twelfth-century Gothic-style church.

St. Matthew's Anglican Church, The Glebe

In 1898, when Ottawa had a population of just 58,000, a little group of Church of England followers founded a parish known as St. Matthew's in the expanding south part of town known as the Glebe. It was the first parish created in the new Anglican Diocese of Ottawa. The parishioners built a small, wood-frame church just west of Bank Street. Prior to the building of the new church, the first service in the parish was held on January 9, 1898. Work on the new church began in the spring and was finished by early summer. Painted a light grey-blue, it had white trim around tall, narrow windows.

The story of St. Matthew's Anglican Church is intertwined with the growth of the Glebe itself. By the early 1900s and within a few years of each other, all major Christian denominations had established churches in the area. Population growth required more churches. By 1920, the Glebe had a population of around 10,000, and little St. Matthew's had grown to be the largest congregation in the Anglican Diocese of Ottawa.

By 1920, the church was free of debt.

It was against this backdrop that in the late 1920s the parishioners and their fifth rector, the Irish-born Canon Robert Jefferson, made plans to build a much larger church and parish hall at a cost of $250,000. In those days that was a staggering amount. The church was constructed and the impressive new stone edifice opened its doors just before Christmas Day 1930.

Designed by Cecil Burgess, a well-known Ottawa architect, the building's Gothic Revival style stone structure was described by the *Ottawa Journal* as "architecturally a triumph." The beautiful new church could seat 1,100 and accommodate a choir of sixty. When one visits St. Matthew's one is impressed with the beautiful stained glass windows and the wooden-frame structure of the roof supports.

The Glebe's St. Matthew's Anglican Church sits in much the same location as its predecessor between what are now First and Glebe avenues.

St. Matthew's, the Anglican Church in the Glebe.

St. Patrick's Basilica, Centretown

Intimately connected to the history of Ottawa, St. Patrick's is the oldest English-language Roman Catholic parish in Ottawa. A committee was formed in 1828 to look into the building of a church but no action resulted. Due to the large Irish immigration to Ottawa in 1852, a small stone Methodist church was purchased for $200, renovated and blessed on May 31. In 1864, seven lots on what is now Nepean Street were purchased from the heirs of Colonel By. This land became the site of the present St. Patrick's Church and construction began in 1869. The original architect was Augustus Laver, of Fuller and Laver, the architects of the East and West blocks of the Parliament Buildings. When construction was disrupted, King Arnoldi took over. On October 6, 1872, the cornerstone was blessed by Bishop Guigues and laid by Prime Minister Macdonald, who also left a donation to the building fund.

The shell of the building was completed by 1873, and the first mass was held on St. Patrick's Day. The church at that time was described in its present website history as having "bare walls, gaunt looking rafters, and seats of the plainest class." Other additions and improvements continued to be added through 1898 and beyond. On St. Patrick's Day, 1995, the church was given the status of a minor basilica, a title conferred on churches of historical or architectural importance that are prominent in their community. Today St. Patrick's remains one of the most beautiful stone churches in Ottawa.

St. Patrick's Basilica is located in the oldest English-language parish in Ottawa.

St. Paul's-Eastern United Church, Sandy Hill

There has been a church on the corner of Cumberland Street and Daly Avenue for 160 years. The first church, Knox Presbyterian, was built in 1845. The congregation grew, and the present building was built in 1889. Since 1925, this building has been known as St. Paul's-Eastern United Church, the joining of the congregations of Eastern Methodist Church and St. Paul's Presbyterian Church.

The architect was R.S. Bagley of Cleveland, Ohio. He built churches in almost all parts of Canada and the United States. He is perhaps best known as the designer of Massey Hall in Toronto. St. Paul's is a wonderful example of a church in the Romanesque style very popular in the 1880s and 1890s. The church's website history notes that it was built of "native rock in random coursed face work with dressed trimmings. The church is amphi-theater [sic] in plan, sloping up every way from the pulpit with circular seating all finished in native wood. The windows will be ornamental stained glass." In 1916, due to the challenges of the sandy soil of Sandy Hill, the prominent corner tower had become unsafe and it had to be shortened, and Baronial qualities with the exaggerated corner turret and tourelles (smaller decorative turets) were taken down. A permanent roof was erected above the bell platform, and there have been no changes to the structure of the corner tower since.

In 1910, Mrs. Katherine Cummings made a gift of a beautiful Casavant three-manual pipe organ to the congregation; it has been providing the music ever since.

For safety reasons, the top of the St. Paul's-Eastern United Church's steeple had to be removed.

St. Paul's Lutheran Church, Sandy Hill

St. Paul's Lutheran Church is located on Wilborn Street. It is a beautiful stone church, showing the ramparts that form an integral part of the construction. This is one of a few churches in the region that exhibit this type of construction.

The stone ramparts of St. Paul's Lutheran Church.

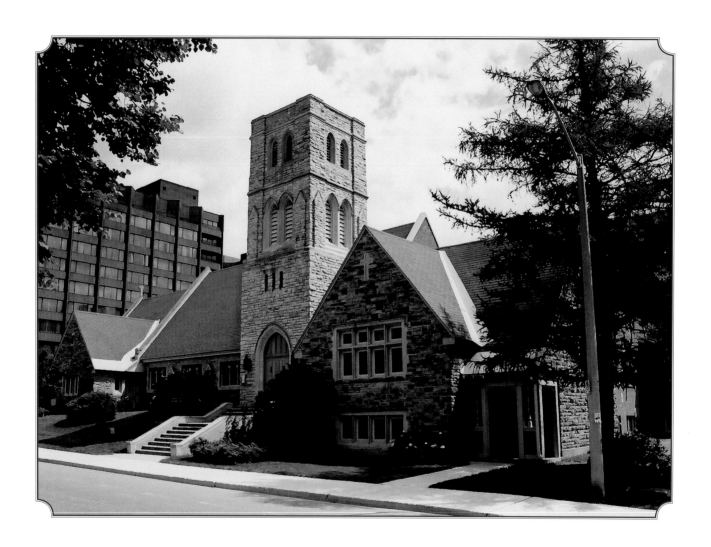

St. Peter's Lutheran Church, Centretown

St. Peter's Lutheran Church was established in 1910. The first building was erected on Lyon Street and dedicated on Easter Sunday in 1914. The early members were predominantly of European origin, whether residents of Ottawa, recent immigrants, or arrivals from neighbouring towns and rural communities.

After many years of financial hardship and difficulties, the congregation gradually increased and outgrew its church building. The present building was dedicated in 1954. It is situated on Ottawa's ceremonial route and overlooks the Garden of the Provinces, the Ottawa River, and the Gatineau Hills. St. Peter's is an Ottawa landmark, designed in traditional Gothic style. The sandstone was cut from the same quarry as stone used for the Parliament Buildings.

The most significant interior features are the Casavant organ, installed in 1977, and a cycle of stained glass windows, created by Canadian artist Russell Goodman between 1985 and 1993. The windows focus on the life of Christ and the Lutheran heritage.

St. Peter's Lutheran Church overlooks the Garden of the Provinces in Ottawa.

St. Theresa Roman Catholic Church, Centretown

St. Theresa Roman Catholic Church is a relatively new church by comparison to many of the stone churches. It was constructed from a dark red brick and trimmed with contrasting red granite from a previous house on the property. The church forms an interesting contrast to all the other churches contained in this book. The parish was originally part of St. Patrick's Parish. It is located at the corner of Somerset and Cartier streets, not far from the Rideau Canal. The church was blessed in August 1930.

The dark red brick and granite of St. Theresa Roman Catholic Church make an interesting contrast.

PART TWO

Churches of Fitzroy, Goulbourn, Huntley, Torbolton, and March Townships in Ottawa West

St. John's Anglican Church, Antrim

From about 1869, services were held in the Fitzroy schoolhouse before St. John's Anglican Church was erected in 1873 on land donated by Mr. John Wilson for a church and burial ground. Bishop J. Travers Lewis consecrated St. John's, Antrim, on December 19, 1888. The exterior of the church and rectory were painted, and the church interior was renovated in the period from 1917 to 1918. In 1961, St. John's was completely redecorated inside. The centennial of St. John's Anglican Church was celebrated in 1973.

St. John's Anglican Church in a peaceful winter scene.

Christ Church Anglican, Ashton

Ashton is a small village on the western boundary of the City of Ottawa and located forty-five kilometres from downtown Ottawa. Ashton was first settled in 1818 by ex-soldiers from Ireland, Scotland, and England after the war of 1812, when the area was still virgin forest. Ashton became a thriving community in the nineteenth century, with a grist mill, blacksmith shops, hotels, general stores, tailors, and shoemakers. The construction of the railway and highway bypasses resulted in businesses moving away. Ashton has remained much as it is now for nearly one hundred years.

Ashton village, although small in population, has four churches, two of which are still used regularly. The first Anglican services were held in private homes by clergy from Richmond. Christ Church was built in 1845, from local limestone, by carpenter John Shore, and stonemason John Bobier, whose families continue to remain active in the community. Since 1887, Christ Church has been on its own as a self-supporting single-point parish. The rectory was built in 1891. The smaller original church has been restored and is now used as a part of the adjacent cemetery.

Left: The original Ashton Anglican Church was built in 1845 from limestone cut from the bed of the Jock River and hauled by oxcart to Ashton. The church was restored around 2005.

Above: The current Ashton Anglican Church

Melville Presbyterian Church, Ashton

Melville Presbyterian (now used as a private residence), was one of four churches in Ashton, Ontario. The church building dates back to 1852, although the building was enlarged and completely renovated in 1879. It is estimated that the congregation actually goes back to 1843. The Melville Presbyterian congregation eventually became associated with the Appleton congregation. At the time of church union that resulted in the formation of the United Church of Canada in 1925, changes were made and services were rotated annually with the Ashton United Church (Ashton Methodist Church). Rotating services continued until 1940. The stone Melville Presbyterian church was then used as a meeting place for the community until it was eventually sold. The present owner has seen fit to reinstall the steeple, which for a few years rested on the ground. One wonders if one day this beautiful church structure will eventually see a new congregation.

The former Melville Presbyterian Church is now a wonderful place to call home.

Bells Corners United Church, Bells Corners

Ministry in the Bells Corners area began in the early 1820s when circuit ministers visited with local families. In 1851, the first regular ministry of the Presbyterian Church began in Bells Corners. In 1853, a Union Church was built by the Anglicans, Methodists, and Presbyterians on the present site of the Bells Corners Union Cemetery. It was the only building to survive the great fire of 1870. The Presbyterians bought out the interests of the other congregations and in 1898 built the Drummond Church on what is now known as Robertson Road, using some of the stone from the demolished church. In 1925, this Presbyterian congregation joined the United Church of Canada and became part of the Britannia-Fallowfield circuit of the newly formed church.

In 1958, Bells Corners United Church (BCUC) became a separate charge and was served by supply ministers. The year 1960 brought great changes. It marked the call of the first full-time ordained minister to BCUC and the planning for the present church building, which began in the fall. Construction started in the spring of 1962, and the new sanctuary, offices, and hall were dedicated on December 2, 1962.

The planning for the second stage of the building program began in 1965. A decision was made in the fall of 1967, and a building committee began its work. This resulted in the construction of the northern wing in the summer of 1969 and dedication that October 15. In 2005, the congregation agreed to the addition of a new entrance to the church building and renovation of the existing narthex and balcony.

Left: The new entry to Bells Corners United Church was officially dedicated on June 4, 2006.

Above: The original Drummond Church (now a spa).

St. James the Apostle Anglican Church, Carp

During the period between the founding of Christ Church and the building of St. John's Anglican Church, a terrible catastrophe in the form of the Great Fire of 1870 destroyed a vast area, including the rectory beside Christ Church. In her *Early History of St. James Church, Parish of Huntley*, Helen Rivington writes: "After the great fire of 1870 people and businesses gravitated towards Carp Village. To accommodate the people, in this new centre, services were held in the Orange Hall in the late 1870s."

Finally, in 1889, both Christ Church and St. John's were firmly ensconced, and St. James the Apostle was constructed. As noted in Rivington's history, "Arthur Johnston and Jack Lett drew stone from a quarry on the Johnston farm (later George Dolan Farm). The cornerstone and sills were brought in from Carleton Place. The church is a model of Gothic construction. Windows are recessed 20 inches into the walls."

St. James was consecrated in 1892. Many of the original families who worshipped there in those first days continue to be represented by members of today's congregation. The atmosphere of continuity and familiarity is felt everywhere in this beautiful church.

St. James the Apostle Anglican Church is located adjacent to the Carp Agricultural Fair Grounds.

St. Michael's Roman Catholic Church, Corkery

Prior to 1837 the parishioners of this mission were served by priests from nearby Bytown, who held services in people's homes. In 1837, a small wooden church was built to serve the needs of the community. The church soon outgrew the 20- by 30-foot building even with a 15-foot addition, which was added in 1845. In 1851, a beautiful stone rectory was built, which resulted in making the wooden church seem too modest. When the little wooden church burned down in 1864, the congregation seized the opportunity to build a new stone church, which was ready by that fall. The church was consecrated under the name of St. Michael on February 26, 1865. Unfortunately, the settling of the church the following year caused damage, and the walls had to be reinforced with iron rods.

St. Michael's is tucked in behind the trees just off Highway 44.

St. Mary's Anglican Church, Dunrobin

Nestled in a peaceful, forested setting on the north side of the 6th Line of March ("6th Line Road"), the present grey stone St. Mary's Anglican Church dates from 1909.

The original church building was erected in 1829 on the south shore of the Ottawa River, a short distance away at historic Pinhey's Point, making this church one of the very oldest and most historically significant Christian congregations in the entire Eastern Ontario/Ottawa Valley region.

When the stone walls of the original church building began to crumble in the early 1900s, the congregation decided to rebuild inland at the present more central and convenient location on what had quickly become the area's main road.

Today's St. Mary's draws its membership from both long-established pioneer and farming families — some of whose ancestors came to the March Township area 180 or more years ago — as well as from newer families who moved out to this beautiful rural area from within the city in more recent times.

St. Mary's Anglican Church on an autumn day in Dunrobin.

St. Paul's Anglican Church, Dunrobin

Situated at the main crossroads in the Village of Dunrobin where Thomas Dolan Parkway and Dunrobin Road intersect, St. Paul's Anglican Church was built in 1896 by local people who wanted a closer-to-home church of their own. They used stone drawn mostly from a nearby quarry, with ornamental pieces being hauled in all the way from Carleton Place.

One of the area's smaller churches, St. Paul's Anglican Church congregation has the reputation as a warm, welcoming, and friendly Christian family. Its doors are open to newcomers and visitors alike.

St. Paul's Anglican Church is a small rural church situated in Dunrobin.

Fallowfield United Church, Fallowfield

As indicated in its website, "Fallowfield treasures its rural roots," the cornerstone of Fallowfield United, then a Methodist church, was laid in place in June 1886 by Canada's first prime minister, Sir John A. Macdonald (then the serving member for Carleton), an honour not every church can claim. Previous to this date, the congregation had worshipped in another frame structure on the same site since 1868. The original building was shared by the Methodists and Presbyterians, who later built their own building next door.

On June 25, 1925, with the formation of the United Church of Canada, the Methodist building became Fallowfield United Church. As indicated in the *Heritage Tour of Nepean* brochure, "The slender sham buttresses and a delicate spire distinguish this church as belonging to the Picturesque Style. Elements such as the pointed arch openings and lancet windows demonstrate that this style incorporates decorative features of Gothic origin."

Today Fallowfield United warmly and enthusiastically embraces its present and its future.

The welcoming Fallowfield United Church stands on a hill in Fallowfield.

St. Patrick's Roman Catholic Church, Fallowfield

Diocesan records make reference to a "small wooden chapel" that was built in 1833. The chapel was known as the "Mission of Nepean," and priests from Bytown and St. Philip's Parish in Richmond, Ontario, conducted the services there.

The mission was built from logs cut in the Fallowfield area, and its purpose was to serve parishioners who otherwise would have travelled a great distance by horse and wagon (or sleigh, in wintertime) to attend Sunday mass in either Richmond or Bytown.

There was no resident priest appointed to serve the community nor was any one person or family designated to keep up the structure of the wooden chapel. A citizens' committee was formed to oversee the construction of a new church to replace the log chapel. The new structure was to be a simple stone building.

A large crowd was on hand on October 21, 1866, when St. Patrick's Roman Catholic Church was first dedicated and blessed. The new church had already cost 972 Louis (the currency of France at the time) before the interior was close to being finished. The completed church, with dimensions measuring 73 feet long and 40 feet wide, is constructed of stone and well-finished inside.

On Sunday, June 12, 1966, the one hundredth anniversary of the parish of St. Patrick's Church, Fallowfield, was celebrated. Today, almost 150 years after it was blessed, St. Patrick's stands as a beautiful memorial to the parishioners who had the foresight to build this stone structure.

St. Patrick's Roman Catholic Church is situated in the village of Fallowfield.

St. Andrew's United Church, Fitzroy Harbour

The first church and school in Fitzroy Township were established by Charles Shirreff in 1832 in a log building on the site of the present St. Andrew's United Church. In 1858, Reverend Mr. Henderson began to devote his energies to building a substantial stone church, which is the current building at Fitzroy Harbour. Church union that resulted in the formation of the United Church of Canada in 1925 helped to strengthen the congregation. In 2008, St. Andrew's celebrated its 150th anniversary.

St. Andrew's United Church on a bright spring day in Fitzroy Harbour.

St. George's Anglican Church, Fitzroy Harbour

St. George's, located in the village of Fitzroy Harbour, began services in 1863, but the actual story of the church starts in 1852 when Alexander Shirreff donated land to the Anglican congregation. Construction began in 1857 when it is recorded that £1,000 would be required to erect the building. The records show that by the year 1863, the foundation with walls but no roof had taken shape at a recorded cost of $2,000. There were no pews and no heat. It wasn't until 1872 that the building was considered complete.

Major renovations had been recorded in the 1950s and the church hall was added in 1968, but it was not until 1981 that the belfry and spire were erected. In 1988, the congregation's 135th anniversary year, extensive repair and enhancement work were undertaken. Then in the year 2000 the original stained glass was cleaned and restored, rendering it in good shape for another hundred years. At the same time the stone work of the weather-beaten building was repointed.

St. George's Anglican Church in the winter.

St. Michael's Roman Catholic Church, Fitzroy Harbour

St. Michael's Roman Catholic Church, built around 1860, is one of three churches to be found in Fitzroy Harbour, a small community endowed with wonderful churches.

St. Michael's Roman Catholic Church on a bright winter's day in Fitzroy Harbour.

St. John's Anglican Church, March

St. John's is one of three Anglican churches in the parish of March. All three were constructed of local quarried stone and are a total of almost 350 years old. St. John's is the oldest, its cornerstone being laid on July 22, 1839. St. Paul's was built during 1896 opposite Younghusband's Store in Dunrobin. St. Mary's was built later in 1906 and is located on the Sixth Line Road near the Thomas A. Dolan Parkway.

It took almost a full year to complete the construction of St. John's Church, and the first service held there was on April 15, 1840. This service was the wedding for two local people from March — William Hedley and Bridget Younghusband. William became the church warden from 1866 to 1868 and both he and Bridget are buried in St. John's cemetery.

This magnificent church was built without the title to the land being secure. (Imagine doing that today!) It wasn't until Horace Pinhey (Pinhey's Estate) stepped in five years later that the title was secured. St. John's Church is also the biggest Anglican church in the entire territory formerly known as March Township and one of the oldest churches of any denomination in the Ottawa Valley. Erected in the late 1830s by some of this area's earliest pioneer settlers, the simple rectangular building's original outer walls were formed from locally quarried stone carted to the site by its faithful founders, and still stand to this day.

Funding was a prevalent issue during the mid-1800s. The church needed pews and these were bought by the parishioners. After purchasing the pews, the holders could then participate in decision making. All of this is somewhat akin to a company raising capital by issuing shares.

The years passed and, by 1913, a telephone was installed in the rectory by the Monk Rural Telephone Company (which is now part of Bell Canada). The modernizing didn't stop there because in 1926 another hi-tech innovation was realized — electric lights! The rapid pace continued when a garage was added to the rectory in 1939.

In 1958, a basement was excavated in order to make way for a new oil furnace. This was a major improvement over the older wood furnace, which was quite insufficient on cold days. Although not a feat of engineering by modern standards, the excavation was completely done by hand! Apparently, everyone helped in this project, including the local sheriff and his sons. Shovels were used to dig the basement, and the excavated earth was placed into buckets and pulled up by rope through a hole in the floor. The excavated earth was placed on a wagon, again by hand.

Four years later, in 1962, the old reed foot-pump organ was replaced by a modern Baldwin electronic organ, a gift to the church from Mr. Claude Riddell, in memory of his wife.

St. John's Anglican Church is now surrounded by homes in Kanata.

Christ Church Anglican, Carp Road, Ottawa West

Christ Church is the oldest original church in the area, and worship within its walls offers an experience steeped in history. In 1819, John Cavanaugh from County Tipperary, Ireland, settled in the wilderness that was wooded Huntley Township. He was Huntley's very first settler. Gradually other hardy settlers joined him there. Cavanaugh felled the first tree in Huntley Township and lived in a dugout in the ground, covered with trees, until he had built a shanty. After nearly twenty years of perseverance, John Cavanaugh deeded five chains, seventeen links (approximately one acre) of his farm land to the Bishop of Quebec for an English church to be built. Suzanne Thompson observed in her article, "Early History of Christ Church, Parish of Huntley," that "included in the deed was the stipulation that 'the above John Cavanaugh was to have pew No. 1 on the south side of the said church.'" Today this pew is still used by the Cavanaugh family.

A meeting was held at the home of Arthur Hopper, who owned the first store in Huntley Township. Suzanne Thompson notes: "At this meeting it was decided that the stone church would be built and it would be 50 feet by 30 feet by 19 feet high. Mr. A. Thomas Christie was given the contract. The stone was supplied by W.B. Bradley and came from nearby Bradley's Creek just two miles away." Christ Church was completed in November 1838. The three-foot-thick stone walls have certainly stood the test of time.

During the period between the founding of Christ Church and the building of St. John's Anglican Church, the Great Fire of 1870 destroyed a vast area, including the rectory beside Christ Church (the stone church survived). After the Great Fire the people and businesses gravitated to Carp village where a new rectory and businesses were at "The Corner" in the village of Carp on land that is now the centre of the Carp Agricultural Fair Grounds.

CHRIST CHURCH 1838

This handsome stone church, in the style of the early Gothic Revival, was built by A. Thomas Christie on land donated by John Cavanagh, one of Huntley township's earliest landholders. Aided by a substantial contribution from Colonel Arthur Lloyd, a veteran of the Napoleonic Wars who had settled in neighbouring March township, the building was completed in 1838. The earliest Anglican settlers were served by missionaries posted in Hull and subsequently in March. The union of the Huntley and March parishes continued until the appointment of the Reverend James Godfrey as Rector of Huntley in 1853. Although the interior has been extensively altered, the building stands as a memorial to the original Anglican settlers.

Erected by the Archaeological and Historic Sites Board.

Left: Christ Church Anglican is the oldest original church in the area.

Above: The historic plaque for Christ Church Anglican located on the Carp Road.

St. Isidore Roman Catholic Church, Ottawa West

A chapel was built in 1836 to serve the Roman Catholic community in March Township. In 1883, "The Mission of March" was renamed "St. Isidore." A stone church was built in 1887 and blessed by Archbishop Duhamel on October 9, 1887. In 1891, a 740-pound bell was purchased and christened "St. Anne." In 1922, electricity came to St. Isidore at a cost of $974 for wiring and fixtures for both the church and the rectory. In 1924, the first telephone bill was paid for the year at a cost of $20.28. In 1934, the installation of the stained glass windows was organized by Father Philip C. Harris, and the beautiful statue of the Blessed Virgin Mary was installed on the front lawn of the rectory in 1946.

In 1961, a new organ was purchased at a cost of $1,595, and around this time, a beautiful lighted cross was installed in the steeple by Ed and Laura Kennedy. In 1987, the one hundredth anniversary of the church was celebrated.

To accommodate the growing population in the area, a decision was made in 2010 to take down the beautiful stone church, while retaining important parts of it to incorporate in the new church; it was a decision not taken lightly. The old stone church was in need of repairs, which would be more than could be reasonably afforded by the parish. The less expensive route would be construction of a new church on the same site at a cost of 5.5 million dollars. How times have changed!

About forty panels of stained glass from the old church were incorporated in the new arched windows. The 740-pound bell, originally hauled up high by a team of horses, was kept and re-installed in a new spire that replicates the old steeple. It will be sounded manually in the future.

Left: The new St. Isidore Roman Catholic Church officially opened January 14, 2012.

Above: The original St. Isidore Roman Catholic Church was demolished in 2010.

123

St. Thomas Anglican Church, Stittsville

The first St. Thomas Anglican Church was born before Confederation in a flourishing little village known as Rathwell's Corners, situated south of Stittsville at the junction of the 9th Line (Flewelleyn Road) and the Huntley Road.

It was here in 1866 that landowner Thomas McCaffery decided to donate some of his property for the building of a church. He gave "thirty square yards of land for building the Church of St. Thomas belonging to the Protestant Episcopal Church of Canada."

The little church prospered, and by 1873 was free of debt when it was consecrated by the Right Reverend John Travis Lewis, Bishop of Ontario. An adjoining burial ground had also been established and a number of Goulbourn's pioneers rest there.

The community where the church stood changed its name to Stanley's Corners in the 1870s. The church building was enlarged in 1914 with the addition of a chancel at the west end. The pews of solid wood were used for nearly a hundred years, and beautiful stained glass windows were added over the years. St. Thomas remained part of the Richmond parish until 1961 when the parish of Stittsville was created.

Late in the afternoon on a beautiful summer's day in June 1964, a severe electrical storm swept through the Stittsville area. As the lightning flashed, it struck the tall steeple of the little white church standing alone on its rise just south of today's Stittsville. The steeple caught fire and soon the flames had spread to the ceiling of the church with its insulation of wood shavings. Through the heroic efforts of many members of the congregation and community, eight of nine wonderful stained glass windows were saved along with many of the church records, the church organ, and many of the vestments. The names and memories of many of the ancestors of the current St. Thomas family live on in the 134-year-old parish through the century-old memorial stained glass windows saved from the fire. The historic windows are now located in the present church building at Carleton and Main streets, the third church to serve this congregation. In addition, the original bell from the little white church on the hill can be seen in the bell tower of the present church, now well protected from lightning by lightning rods.

The present St. Thomas Anglican Church in Stittsville.

Stittsville United Church, Stittsville

In 1819, Ezra Healey, a faithful Methodist saddle-bag preacher, began to establish classes of approximately twenty members each in the forests and wilderness between the Rideau and Ottawa rivers. In 1824, George and Mary Argue and their four sons, William, Robert, Andrew, and John, established a homestead on lot 21, concession 11, in the Township of Goulbourn, approximately one mile west of the village of Stittsville. When the family home was completed, the neighbours gathered to give thanks to God. This was the first Methodist service ever held in Goulbourn Township. When Ezra Healey reached the Stittsville area, he placed the Methodist adherents under the leadership of the aforementioned George Argue, along with James Wilson and Archibald Magee.

It was not, however, until 1845, when William Magee granted to the trustees of the Methodist congregation one acre of land on which the current church now stands, that a permanent church was established. That first building, constructed of logs, was known as the Magee Chapel. In 1847, a stone building, first known as the Argue Chapel and subsequently as the Wesley Methodist Church, was built about one hundred yards (ninety metres) east of the existing building. The remains of the foundation of that stone church can still be seen in the church cemetery. Its structure was rather crude, with round rather than quarried stones used to create the outside walls. By 1883, the stone building was replaced by the "Brick Church," which met the needs of the growing congregation for the next seventy years; the brick building still forms a significant part of the current sanctuary. When the union of certain Methodist, Congregationalist, and Presbyterian groups created the United Church of Canada in 1925, Wesley Methodist became Stittsville United Church.

From 1883 until 1963, the brick church was heated by two wood stoves located on either side of the main entrance. A long string of pipes ran from each stove to the front of the church. Needless to say, church service in the winter was most likely an invigorating experience. A particular story recalls that Mrs. Margaret MacDougall, the church organist for more than forty years from the 1940s through the 1980s, often led the service with fingers barely able to feel the keys. Another story, again involving Marg, was that of a church mouse; the mouse became so persistent that Mrs. MacDougall had to wear her overshoes while playing the organ until the little visitor was caught. As well, bees in the belfry — including dripping honey — form a part of the history of Stittsville United.

A view across the cemetery adjacent to Stittsville United Church.

St. Thomas Anglican Church, Woodlawn

A frame church was being used at Torbolton (later called Woodlawn) by 1874. St. Thomas Anglican Church was consecrated on September 20, 1882, by Bishop J. Travers Lewis. In 1915, the present stone St. Thomas Anglican Church was built to replace the old structure, which was moved to the back of the lot and used until the new one was completed. The cornerstone of the new church was laid by Bishop John Charles Roper on July 1, 1915. The Bishop consecrated St. Thomas, Woodlawn, on December 14 of the same year. Land was donated in 1925 by Mr. James Brown for a burial ground, which was consecrated by Bishop E.S. Reed in September of 1955. On November 3, 1965, the centennial of St. Thomas and the fiftieth anniversary of the building and consecration of the church were celebrated. Since 1985, St. Thomas, Woodlawn, along with St. George's, Fitzroy Harbour, have been part of the parish of Fitzroy Harbour.

St. Thomas Anglican Church is a country church in Woodlawn.

PART THREE

Churches of the Madawaska and Mississippi River Valleys

Almonte United Church, Almonte

Almonte United Church occupies a significant location in the centre of the town of Almonte. The original worshippers for this congregation came from the Auld Kirk, circa 1834–1836. The present building was constructed in 1861. The cornerstone was laid in 1865 after the Presbyterians attending the Auld Kirk Church realized that the centre of activity in the area was going to be in the village of Almonte.

The architecture has been described as classic Scottish and was carefully preserved during the numerous renovations that have taken place over the years. It wasn't until 1951 that the two United Church congregations of Bethany and Trinity joined and started worshipping together in the present Almonte United Church.

Almonte United Church is located in the centre of Almonte.

Auld Kirk, Almonte

The Auld Kirk, an attractive example of an early form of Gothic Revival architecture, was constructed in the period from 1835 to 1836 on land obtained from John Mitchell, one of Ramsay Township's earliest settlers. Built by the local congregation of the Established Church of Scotland, it was also attended by Presbyterians from adjoining townships. The early settlers of Ramsay were visited by ministers from Drummond and Beckwith, but in 1834, the first resident minister, the Reverend John Fairburn, was inducted. In January 1864, during the ministry of the Reverend John McMorine (1846–1867), a new church was opened in nearby Almonte. Although little used since then, the Auld Kirk stands as a memorial to the pioneer Presbyterian settlers.

Left: A memorial to the pioneer Presbyterian settlers.

Above: The historic plaque at the Auld Kirk.

Holy Name of Mary Roman Catholic Church, Almonte

The physical site of the present Holy Name of Mary Roman Catholic Church was established in 1842, but the early beginnings of this congregation go back as far as 1823. Daniel Shipman made a gift of one-and-a-half acres of land to Father John Hugh McDunagh to enable the building of St. Mary's Mission Church in the community then known as Shipman's Mills. The 33- by 49-foot frame church was constructed in 1842.

On Christmas night, 1868, fire claimed the old wooden church. Immediately, the faithful of the parish joined to raise a new stone church. One parishioner, William Madden, even mortgaged his farm and home for $2,000 to get the work started. The new church was almost twice as large as the old one.

On October 7, 1875, the stone church was consecrated, fifty-two years after the first mass was held in the wilderness of Ramsay Township. Although the parish has historically and formally been called Holy Name of Mary, with references to such in diocesan material dating to the 1930s, the sign on the front of the church was not changed until 1996. A dynamic renewal of the parish and the church renovations to the bell tower and restoration of heritage details in the interior of the church began in 2002, when the large and magnificent stained glass windows were restored.

Holy Name of Mary Roman Catholic Church occupies a prominent location in the town of Almonte.

Reformed Presbyterian Church, Almonte

This beautiful little stone church is situated on a hillside facing the Mississippi River in Almonte. Presbyterian congregations go back to 1827 when families arrived from Scotland. In 1833, this congregation was first organized, but it was not until 1891 that the present church was erected. The Reformed Presbyterian denomination is fairly recent in the Ottawa area and has been expanding since the mid-1980s.

The Reformed Presbyterian Church overlooks the Mississippi River in Almonte.

St. John's Presbyterian Church, Almonte

St. John's Presbyterian Church is situated in the village of Almonte. The church community was established as early as 1845 but had its beginnings in St. Andrew's Presbyterian Church in 1833. The cornerstone of St. John's was laid in 1865, and the centennial was celebrated in 1965.

In 1925, the majority of Almonte Presbyterian Church congregants voted to join the United Church union; however, a minority chose to retain their Presbyterian affiliation and purchased St. John's Presbyterian Church, renovated it, and retained the name.

St. John's Presbyterian Church has been returned to its glory.

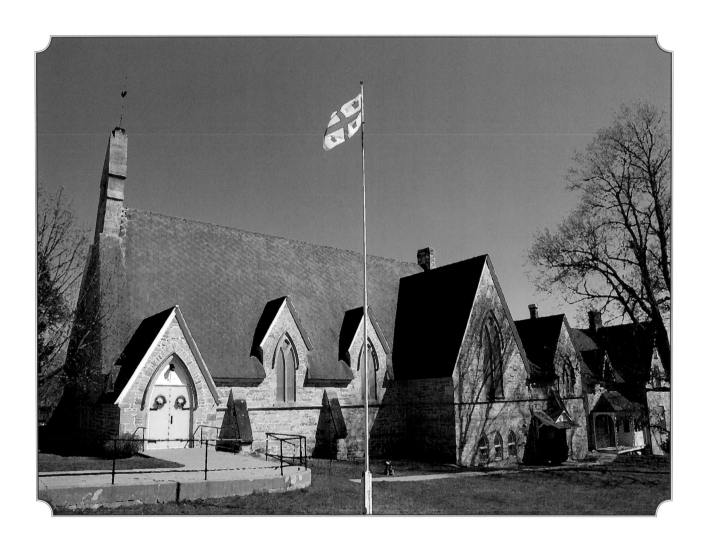

St. Paul's Anglican Church, Almonte

St. Paul's Anglican is a fine stone church beautifully located along the Mississippi River in Almonte. In 1862, St. Paul's was erected in an English Parish Gothic style. The cost of the church building, site, and bell was settled at $3,749. James Rosamond, a representative of one of the twelve founding families, laid the first stone May 7, 1863. The stained glass windows were offered to the glory of God in memory of the twelve founding families. The church was consecrated on St. Peter's Day, June 29, 1864. That year, the rector, Reverend Peter Slade, was paid the princely stipend of $200.

St. Paul's will celebrate its 150th anniversary in 2013.

Prominent Almonte families founded St. Paul's Anglican Church.

Grace St. Andrew's United Church, Arnprior

Grace St. Andrew's United Church is another of the beautiful stone churches to be found in the Ottawa Valley. The "Stone Church," as St. Andrew's Presbyterian Church was known, was built about 1890. The Wesleyan Methodists constructed the brick building called Grace Methodist next to that building in 1894. The two denominations were amalgamated as the United Church in 1925, and Grace St. Andrew's became the sanctuary for the newly formed church community.

The "Stone Church," as Grace St. Andrew's United Church was known.

St. John Chrysostom Roman Catholic Church, Arnprior

S t. John Chrysostom Roman Catholic Church is the largest church in the Parish of Pembroke and certainly one of the most beautiful stone churches in the Ottawa Valley. The beginnings of the parish were as early as 1857. The corner stone was blessed in 1907, and construction of the new church building was begun.

St. John Chrysostom Roman Catholic Church stands on the Madawaska River in Arnprior.

St. Andrew's United Church, Burnstown

As you approach Burnstown from the south, you come across a long bridge spanning the Madawaska River. On the far north shore ahead, one sees a tall white spire. That is the spire of a beautiful red brick church that is St. Andrew's United. The St. Andrew's congregation has served the community for over 150 years. The 150th anniversary of the congregation was celebrated in 1999, and the one hundredth anniversary of this church building was celebrated the same year. The congregation was originally a Free Kirk congregation, which later became Presbyterian before joining the United Church at the time of church union that resulted in the formation of the United Church of Canada in 1925.

St. Andrew's United Church is located in the beautiful village of Burnstown.

St. Andrew's Presbyterian Church, Carleton Place

St. Andrew's Presbyterian Church community in Carleton Place was founded by Reverend William Bell in 1817. The present St. Andrew's Church was built on land donated by Mr. John Gillies to be used for a church, meeting house, and cemetery. In 1886, the building committee accepted the proposal of architect S.R. Bagley for a new church to be constructed of native stone with Beckwith stone trimmings at a cost of $8,000. At an actual cost of $10,150, church construction was begun in 1886 and finished by November 1887.

St. Andrew's Church is another of the Presbyterian churches started by Reverend Bell.

St. James Anglican Church, Carleton Place

The Anglican parish of St. James was founded in 1834. St. James is a beautiful stone church situated on the border of the Mississippi River in the town of Carleton Place.

The structure of the church's interior is very unique in that the exposed wooden timbers, which hold up the roof, add to the beauty of the interior. The church is noted for the beauty of the stained glass windows, which one must see to appreciate. It is interesting that the church, which celebrated its 175th anniversary in recent years, still owns 200 acres known as the St. James Woods and operates the St. James Cemetery, which has been said to be one of the most beautiful private cemeteries in Canada. These properties were part of a land grant "Clergy Lands" granted by the government to Protestant churches under the 1791 Constitution.

St. James Anglican Church in Carleton Place sits adjacent to the Mississippi River.

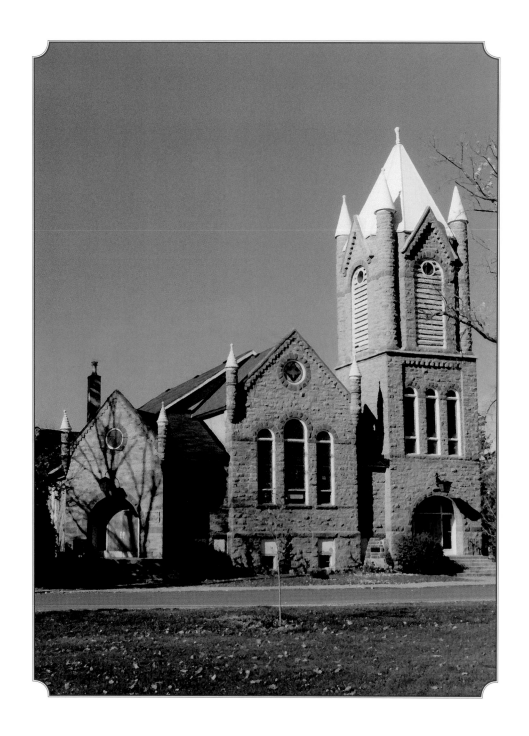

Zion-Memorial United Church, Carleton Place

The present Zion-Memorial United Church was built by the Methodist Congregation of Carleton Place, and the cornerstone of the church was laid in May of 1888. The bell was installed in 1889 and the Casavant organ in 1913. In 1925, the Congregational, Methodist, and Presbyterian congregations merged to form the United Church. In Carleton Place, St. Andrew's Presbyterian Church and the Methodist congregations voted to merge and to worship in the Methodist Church. The newly united congregations adopted the name Memorial Park United for its church building.

Memorial Park United Church was struck by fire in February 1954, leaving only the bell tower and steeple standing. The church was rebuilt and opened in May 1955. In the '60s, discussions about amalgamation were restarted; finally in May 1966, Zion United and Memorial Park United decided to unite and agreed on the new name Zion-Memorial United Church. As recorded in the *History of Zion-Memorial United Church*, "In the late 1990s, the original bell in the steeple fell silent because an inspection revealed that almost 110 years of service and corrosion had left the bell tower in a condition too dangerous to be used. The old manual arrangement was dismantled, the original bell mounted in a fixed position, and an electronically controlled hammer was installed to simulate the bell being rung." Since 2001, the bell has been calling members to worship and also peals to mark noon every day.

Zion-Memorial United Church in Carleton Place.

St. John's Anglican Church, Innisville

St. John's Anglican Church is situated on Highway 7 at the turn to Ferguson Falls, in Innisville, just west of Carleton Place. St. John's is a beautiful, solid stone church with a rounded chancel and square tower. This design is typical of many of the churches of the time. The church community's origins date back to before 1911. St. John's Anglican Church was built in 1911 and celebrated its one hundredth anniversary in 2011.

Many commuters pass by St. John's Anglican Church every day.

St. Andrew's United Church, Lanark

St. Andrew's traces its first activity back to 1820. The first church was built in 1823 and was a 26- by 36-foot structure with eight windows. The present church was built on the original site in 1860 and the cornerstone was laid in 1862.

The building was finished in a Gothic style with a high steeple, which was later removed.

The cost of construction was £1,200, an enormous cost, considering that the average Sunday collection plate at the time contained sixty cents, mostly in coppers. In 1898, a horse shed was built and it was this horse shed that saved the church when a disastrous fire occurred in 1959. By being in the path of the fire, the sheds were lost but the church was saved.

St. Andrew's United Church was one of the earliest congregations in the area.

St. Paul's Anglican Church, Lanark

St. Paul's Anglican Church, Lanark, dates back to 1854. This pretty little church stands on a hill just on the outskirts of the village of Lanark.

The rural setting suits St. Paul's Anglican Church.

St. Andrew's United Church, Pakenham

The early origins of the St. Andrew's Church community go back to 1841. Today, St. Andrew's United is noted not only for its different architecture but for the beauty of the stone from which it was built. The limestone came from a local quarry, while the trim is Nova Scotia red limestone. Combined with the red tile roofing, the red limestone gives the church its very distinctive appearance. Described as American Gothic, the building has a 75-foot tower on one end. It is of interest that The Right Honourable Mackenzie Bowell, who subsequently became prime minister of Canada in 1894, attended the laying of the cornerstone in 1891. It seems appropriate that Pakenham has the curved arch bridge that seems to blend with the limestone of this church.

The red limestone trim adorning St. Andrew's United Church came all the way from Nova Scotia.

St. Peter Celestine Roman Catholic Church, Pakenham

St. Peter Celestine Roman Catholic Church strikes anyone familiar with the religious architecture of the Ottawa Valley as being from a quite different tradition. Most Roman Catholic churches built in the area in the last century were in the Gothic-revival style reminiscent of the great cathedrals of medieval Europe. They are characterized by long, high naves lighted by tall, pointed windows. St. John the Baptist Roman Catholic Church in Perth is probably the finest local example of this style. By contrast, St. Peter Celestine is in the Classic style traditional in the southern countries of Europe. Round arches and smaller windows are features. Interior decoration is more important than the windows in this style, which accounts for the elaborate painting inside the sanctuary.

Construction started in 1892 when the first carload of cut stone arrived at Pakenham station from the Montreal Road quarries in April. The digging of the cellar began as soon as the ground thawed that year, so that laying of the foundation could begin in late May 1892. The congregation moved into the new church in 1893.

The church building is in the form of a cross, as is usual. The body of the church, the nave, is the base of the cross. Its arms are the two transepts where the side altars stand, and the top of the cross is the sanctuary. The building, standing on foundation walls 5 feet thick, is 126 feet long and 50 feet wide. The ridgepole of the church is at 62 feet above the church floor while the cross on top of the tower is 138 feet above ground level. Almost everything on the interior remains today as it was finished in 1901.

Mary Cook states in her "Valley Tales" column, published regularly in *Forever Young*, that "many people who are knowledgeable on the subject of churches, have said that everything about this magnificent structure puts it into the class of outstanding and architecturally superb churches in the entire country."

The reader is encouraged to look up the detailed history of St. Peter Celestine Roman Catholic Church. It is rich and informative and shows the power of the people to build a monument to their faith. I encourage you to visit St. Peter Celestine's website.

Situated on a hilltop in Pakenham, St. Peter Celestine Roman Catholic Church stands as built.

PART FOUR

Churches of the Rideau Valley

Christ Church Anglican, Burrett's Rapids

The construction of Christ Church Anglican was begun in 1831 and completed the following year. This framed church was designed in the Gothic style customarily used in churches of that period. The Anglican congregation had been formed around 1822 in this part of Marlborough and Oxford townships, where the earliest settlers on the Rideau had located in 1830. Daniel Burrett had donated land for a church and a burial ground at the rapids bearing his name. In 1834, the church was consecrated as Christ Church.

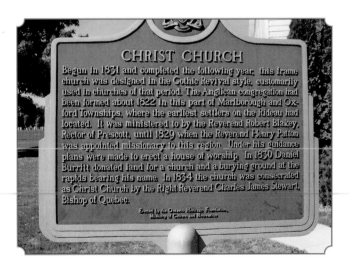

CHRIST CHURCH

Begun in 1831 and completed the following year, this frame church was designed in the Gothic Revival style, customarily used in churches of that period. The Anglican congregation had been formed about 1822 in this part of Marlborough and Oxford Townships, where the earliest settlers on the Rideau had located. It was ministered to by the Reverend Robert Blakey, Rector of Prescott, until 1829 when the Reverend Henry Patton was appointed missionary to this region. Under his guidance plans were made to erect a house of worship. In 1830 Daniel Burritt donated land for a church and a burying ground at the rapids bearing his name. In 1834 the church was consecrated as Christ Church by the Right Reverend Charles James Stewart, Bishop of Quebec.

Erected by the Ontario Heritage Foundation,
Ministry of Culture and Recreation

Left: Christ Church Anglican is a framed church designed in the Gothic style.

Above: The historic plaque at Christ Church Anglican, Burrett's Rapids.

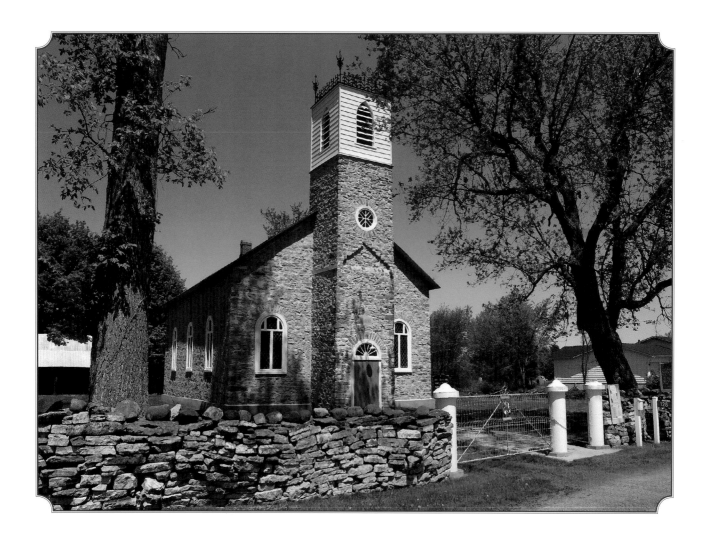

St. James Anglican Church, Franktown

St. James Anglican Church, Franktown, was built in 1822 and is one of the oldest remaining Anglican churches in Eastern Ontario. St. James Centennial Hall consists partly of a small stone structure known as "the Little Hall" built for the King's storehouse in 1818 and 1819. It still stands today and has been used since it was built as a storehouse, school, church, woodshed, and a small hall during its 178-year history. The drive shed, used during the days of the horse and buggy, still stands behind the church.

The original organ, believed to be in the church by 1827, was repaired for the first time in 1877. This fact is recorded on a brass plaque on the back of the organ. The organ was used continually until 1952 when it was wired for electricity. The stained glass windows in St. James Church were shipped from England. Many early relics still remain in the church and are well worth a visit to see.

Left: The driveshed still stands beside St. James Anglican Church.

Above: A historic plaque noting the history of St. James Anglican Church, Franktown.

St. Paul's United Church, Franktown

St. Paul's United Church, a former Presbyterian church in Franktown, traces its origins to 1822 when a church was built on the seventh line of Beckwith Township. While officially known as the Beckwith Presbyterian Congregation in connection with the Church of Scotland, it was known commonly as the "Seventh Line Church." In 1869, Carleton Place was added as a second point. In 1870, the Beckwith church relocated to Franktown and took the name St. Paul's, while the church in Carleton Place took the name St. Andrew's. In 1888, St. Andrew's became a separate congregation. St. Paul's Presbyterian Church entered the United Church in 1925.

The architecture of this church is of particular interest, and the spire catches the eye of the motorist driving through Franktown. The bell tower is unique and at the same time quite similar to the bell tower of St. Andrew's Presbyterian Church in Carleton Place. A historical plaque stands in front of St. Paul's and recognizes the first minister, Reverend George Buchanan.

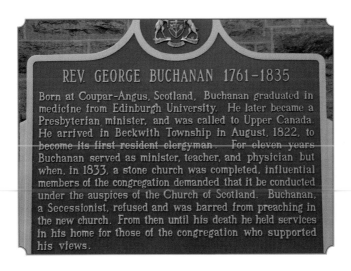

REV. GEORGE BUCHANAN 1761–1835

Born at Coupar-Angus, Scotland, Buchanan graduated in medicine from Edinburgh University. He later became a Presbyterian minister, and was called to Upper Canada. He arrived in Beckwith Township in August, 1822, to become its first resident clergyman. For eleven years Buchanan served as minister, teacher, and physician but when, in 1833, a stone church was completed, influential members of the congregation demanded that it be conducted under the auspices of the Church of Scotland. Buchanan, a Secessionist, refused and was barred from preaching in the new church. From then until his death he held services in his home for those of the congregation who supported his views.

Left: The spire of St. Paul's United Church catches the eye of the motorist passing through Franktown.
Above: The historic plaque at St. Paul's United Church.

Trinity United Church, Kars

Located on the Rideau Valley Drive in the village of Kars, Trinity United is one of three churches in Kars. Trinity United, built in 1895, was originally Wellington Methodist until the church union that resulted in the formation of the United Church of Canada in 1925.

Completed in 1895, the locally quarried stone building was designed in the Gothic Revival style with a mill-cut stone trim reminiscent of an earlier time. Inside are two aisles, a central pulpit platform, and a raised choir loft backed by a large, original stained glass window. The hardwood pews are curved and mounted on sloping floors. Overhead, vee-jointed geometric patterned panels and supporting beams show careful workmanship and the warmth of aged wood. The bell tower contains an 1896 bronze-cast bell that still rings every Sunday morning. Two distinctive front entry porches invite worshippers and village visitors.

At the opening service, after the cornerstone was laid in 1894, Reverend D.S. Chown stood before the congregation and invited them to pray to see if they could find a way to wipe out the $1,500 mortgage. He then asked for pledges and received three of $500 each—a large sum in those days!

Over the years many improvements have been made; drive sheds were built in 1898 as a shelter for horses and vehicles but were torn down in the 1950s. A notable project was the 1975 publication by Audrey Renton of a *History of Trinity United Church, Kars, Ontario* written to mark the fiftieth year of United Church union. It traces the history of Sunday school from 1862 when a Methodist church stood on the site! In 1993, Trinity United Church was designated a Heritage Building by the Rideau Township Local Architectural Conservation Advisory Committee. The one hundredth anniversary of the church building was celebrated in 1995.

Trinity United Church is located on Rideau Valley Drive in the village of Kars.

St. Brigid's Roman Catholic Mission, Manotick

St. Brigid's Roman Catholic Mission was founded as a mission in 1854. In 1858, a small stone church 30 by 40 feet in diameter was built and blessed. It was called St. Brigid's, after the second most popular Irish saint after St. Patrick, and was located halfway between the villages of Osgoode and Manotick on the edge of the Rideau River. This first church was replaced in 1918 after several structural problems were identified. Today the church remains a mission of St. John's Church and serves parishioners from the Manotick area.

St. Brigid's Roman Catholic Mission was founded as a mission in 1854.

St. James the Apostle Anglican Church, Manotick

On July 31, 1875, Moss Kent Dickinson conveyed a lot on the north side of Bridge Street to the Diocese of St. James. The new congregation held its first vestry meeting on May 8, 1876, and a building committee (which included Mr. Dickinson) was immediately struck. No time was wasted; following a second vestry meeting on May 16, architectural plans for the new church were drawn up. Tenders closed on June 27, and a bid of $1,047 was accepted from William Beaman, the son of one of the first three lumbermen in North Gower Township. The contractor received his final payment in 1877, at which time there appears to have been no outstanding debt for the new parish church of St. James the Apostle. On February 22, 1877, the *Ottawa Free Press* stated that "[t]he new Anglican Church in Manotick was opened for public worship on Sunday last. The edifice is beautifully situated near the village, of Gothic style, with open roof, chancel, vestry and porch, painted without and oiled and varnished within, and contains about 200 sittings. It is an ornament to that romantic little village, and a credit to the builders, and the incumbent, the Reverend Mr. O'Loughlin." Changes and developments continued over the years. The first organ was acquired in 1879. After 1896, an enlargement was completed and a bell tower constructed. Electric lights were first turned on in 1926. A full basement was finally completed in 1945. Renovations were carried out on both the church and rectory during the '60s as the parish continued to grow.

The original St. James Church building had served its predominantly rural congregation well, but as the 1980s arrived, it became apparent that the existing structure was not adequate for the needs of the parish. Its fabric was in relatively poor condition and it was difficult to heat in winter. With a growing local population to serve, members of the vestry decided in 1984 that a new and larger church should be built on the same site. A great deal of finishing work for the new church was done by members of the congregation, and as many as possible of the old interior furnishings were incorporated into the new building. The renewed St. James Church was dedicated in 1985 and was consecrated by the Bishop of Ottawa in 1993. In 1998, an addition was built to provide an elevator for handicapped access, as well as new office space and meeting rooms. A visitor to the church will see a traditional but recently built structure, with plaques and stained glass windows hearkening back to an earlier age.

The beauty of St. James the Apostle Church has been restored over the years.

Munster United Church, Munster Hamlet

In 2003, Munster United Church, another example of a small community stone church, celebrated the 180th anniversary of the congregation whose origins go back to 1823. In the period from 1822 to 1823, an American Methodist circuit preacher, Ezra Healy, who had made his way with great difficulty among the settlements, organized classes in many homes. Thomas Shillington, a class leader, built a log church at the road by his laneway. He died in 1840 and was buried in his burial ground, which remains known as "Shillington's Cemetery." In 1877, John Shillington's brother, Thomas Jr., deeded a lot to the Methodist Church where a new stone church was constructed in 1884. Unfortunately, this church burned down in 1891; it was replaced in 1894 by the current stone church. The newer structure houses a bell, imported from Dublin, Ireland, and a beautiful stained glass window, which faces the road. This remains the site of Munster United today.

Munster United is an example of a small rural stone church.

Holy Trinity Anglican Church, North Gower

Holy Trinity Anglican is a beautiful stone church, which I came upon on an excursion to North Gower. The cornerstone of the church was laid on June 25, 1879. The dressed stone for the church was quarried in Goulbourn Township and brought to North Gower by members of the congregation. The rough stone used for the foundation and walls was brought from Hugh Moffat's farm in Marlborough and from the Leach farm in North Gower.

In 2009, the original bell tower was inspected and found to be in need of repair. At great cost to the congregation, the necessary restorations were made, and the bells once again sound in a solid bell tower.

The beautiful stone Holy Trinity Anglican Church is found in North Gower.

North Gower United Church, North Gower

Another beautiful example of the wooden structures built to house our church congregations is North Gower United Church, one of the older churches in the region. Built in 1870 as a Methodist Church, North Gower United has been part of the United Church of Canada since the union that resulted in the formation of the United Church in 1925. It has missed disaster when threatened by fire on several occasions in the late 1800s, 1947, and again in 1967, when the church hall burned.

The building is of frame construction in a classic design fronted by a tower. The tower supports an octagonal belfry and spire over a small-ish entry. The church celebrated its 125th anniversary in 1996. The church has undergone many renovations, which have contributed to maintaining its beauty.

North Gower United Church stands out as one of the beautiful buildings in the village.

St. John the Evangelist Roman Catholic Church, Osgoode

St. John the Evangelist Roman Catholic Church owes its beginnings to Irish immigrants who settled in the area and established a church community. The original church, a 40- by 60-foot structure, was constructed and blessed in 1858.

In 1898, the congregation realized that the wooden building had outlived its usefulness, but it took another twenty years for a new stone church to become a reality. The stone was quarried locally and hauled by horse and sleigh by the parishioners themselves to the Osgoode site. In 1919, the church was blessed. In spite of a fire that caused extensive damage in November 1930, the church was salvaged and repaired for use again by February 1932. The church building stands today as a memorial to the many hard-working parishioners who ensured its survival.

Irish immigrants founded the parish of St. John the Evangelist Roman Catholic Church.

St. John the Evangelist Anglican Church, Oxford Mills

St. John the Evangelist, situated in Oxford Mills near the Rideau River, is a lovely Gothic stone church surrounded by trees. The church was erected in 1871 and celebrated its 125th anniversary in 1996. When one drives through this region of Eastern Ontario, coming upon a beautiful stone church like this makes the drive worthwhile.

St. John the Evangelist Anglican Church is a lovely Gothic stone church in Oxford Mills.

St. Andrew's Presbyterian Church, Perth

Perth was established in 1816 as a military settlement. The Scottish settlers wanted to have the Ordinance of the Gospel among them, so they petitioned the Associate Presbytery of Edinburgh, Scotland, for a minister.

Reverend William Bell arrived in 1817 and held his first service above Adamson's Red Inn on Craig Street. In 1818, he began the construction of a church on the corner of Drummond and Halton streets. Completed in 1819, the church was destroyed by fire in 1867. The bell was saved and later presented to St. Andrew's Presbyterian Church.

In 1830, work was begun on the first St. Andrew's Church at the corner of Drummond and Craig streets, and it was completed in 1833. On March 8, 1898, the final communion was held in this building. A cornerstone for a new church was laid on June 7, 1898. The sanctuary was dedicated on January 29, 1899. This church was destroyed by fire in 1923. Laying of the cornerstone for the current church took place on July 19, 1927. The dedication of St. Andrew's Church at Drummond and North streets was held on March 11, 1928.

Over the years, many changes or additions have been made to the interior, but the exterior of the church remains unchanged.

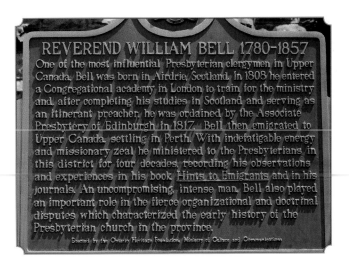

Left: The Presbyterians founded many of the area's churches.

Above: The historic plaque of Reverend William Bell in Perth.

St. James Anglican Church, Perth

Geographically, St. James Anglican Church is almost the most south-westerly parish in the Diocese of Ottawa and in the Deanery of Lanark. The parish was founded in 1816 as a garrison church, and the present building was constructed during the period from 1856 to 1861. In 1836, St. James was granted a Royal Charter by King William IV.

Located at the corner of Drummond and Harvey streets, the church is a sturdy, grey stone structure with a large bell tower. The interior features magnificent stained glass windows and graceful carved wood. The sanctuary seats approximately 400 people.

St. James Anglican Church is a truly beautiful stone structure situated in the historic town of Perth.

St. James Anglican Church in Perth reminds one of many churches found in England.

St. John the Baptist Roman Catholic Church, Perth

A detailed history, *175 Years of Faith: The Story of the Parish of St. John the Baptist, Perth,* outlining the history of the Roman Catholic community in the Perth area was written in 1998. Copies of the book are available at local bookstores and at the back of the church. This in-depth book contains many photographs and copies of written documentation that were retrieved from archives and museums. For anyone researching family histories or attempting to obtain research documents related to the development of faith in Upper Canada, this book is a prime source.

Even though many local history books and even the dedication stone on the main spire say the church was "Erected in 1848," the cornerstone of St. John the Baptist Church was put in place on May 19, 1847. An article from the *Bathurst Courier* published on June 1, 1847, and written by the pastor, outlines the elaborate ceremony that went with the laying of the cornerstone. Construction of the church was a long process. Other articles reveal that the foundations were in place in July of 1843. The historical plaque describes the many firsts and origins of St. John the Baptist.

Left: St. John the Baptist is the first Roman Catholic parish in the Ottawa Valley.

Above: The historic plaque at St. John the Baptist Roman Catholic Church.

St. Paul's United Church, Perth

St. Paul's United was formed in 1926 through the union of Knox Presbyterian and Asbury Methodist congregations, both of which had become United churches the previous year.

Knox Presbyterian Church community was originally formed in 1845 by Reverend William Bell. The Knox congregation built the beautiful, old stone building that now houses St. Paul's United on Gore Street West in 1854. The Asbury Methodist congregation, which had its beginnings in a Methodist circuit established in 1821, built a stone church on Gore Street East in 1884.

In 1926, the combined congregations of Presbyterians and Methodists chose to worship at Knox Presbyterian Church and decided to rename it St. Paul's United Church. As a millennial project, St. Paul's published the book, *St. Paul's United Church, Perth: A Chronicle of 183 Years, 1817–2000*, which details the life and work of the historic church. It can be obtained at the church office.

The stone walls of St. Paul's United Church have seen much over the years.

Prospect United Church, Prospect

The congregation of Prospect United Church actually began to form as early as 1827. The present stone church was built in 1847, with alterations made to the church building in the 1870s. The church also underwent renovations in 1905. The 150th anniversary was celebrated in 1996. The church is little used today but is being maintained for special occasions. Prospect United is another of the older stone churches falling into disuse because of the dwindling numbers of congregants in the area.

Prospect United Church stands between Richmond and Franktown in the village of Prospect.

St. Augustine's Anglican Church, Prospect

St. Augustine's Anglican Church is another of the small stone churches that has fallen on hard times. Built around 1854, the church has not been used for regular services since 1967. Each year, around August 1, a cemetery memorial service is held at St. Augustine's.

Left: St. Augustine's Anglican Church may be small, but it has its beauty.

Above: The brass plaque celebrating St. Augustine's 150th anniversary.

St. Andrew's Presbyterian Church, Richmond

After the war of 1812, Britain undertook plans for colonization in Canada. Many people from Glasgow were chosen and they sailed to Canada around the middle of July 1815. Some settled in Perth. Veterans and others kept arriving, and by September 1816, it was recommended that a new military depot be established in another settlement. A site was chosen, and Richmond was settled by veterans of the 99th Regiment and their families. Part of the Perth settlement agreement was that a Presbyterian minister be provided for the area. Reverend William Bell was chosen for the assignment and arrived in Perth in 1817. Reverend Bell was commissioned to visit Richmond in 1822. In 1884, a brick church was built in Richmond on the same spot as the original building.

Veterans of the 99th Regiment settled in Richmond and established St. Andrew's Presbyterian Church.

St. John's Anglican Church, Richmond

Richmond was the third military settlement of British soldiers, who had seen service in the War of 1812–1814 with the United States. At the end of the war, the soldiers were offered passage to return to England or, along with a pension, a parcel of land to settle in Richmond. Those who accepted became the first settlers of Richmond.

The Parish of Richmond came into being with construction of the first St. John's Church. In 1823, the cornerstone was laid by the local lodge of the "Free Masons" on St. John the Baptist Day, June 24.

The first church was replaced in 1860 by the present church, which is constructed of quarried limestone with a steeply pitched gabled roof and pointed arch windows. It is not known when the first church was torn down, but in the period from 1862 to 1864, it was used as a drill hall. The cornerstone of the first church, bearing the date A.D. 1823, together with the Masonic Emblems, can be seen in the wall near the door at the main entrance of the present church. In June 1961, a historic plaque was erected on the site of the original frame and stone church by the Ontario Archaeological and Historic Sites Board. This memorial plaque, pictured below, commemorates the establishment of St. John's as the first parish and the first church built in Carleton County.

Left: The soldiers who fought in the War of 1812 were important to the establishment of St. John's Anglican Church.
Above: The historic plaque outlining the history of St. John's Anglican Church.

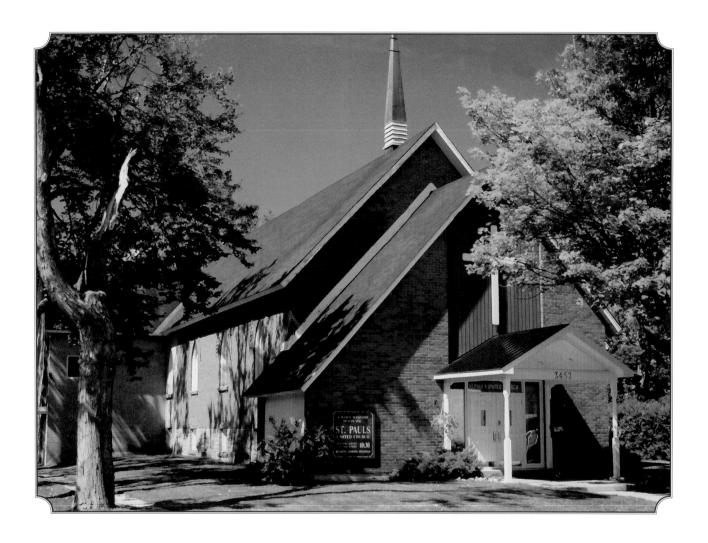

St. Paul's United Church, Richmond

St. Paul's United Church is located on Mc-Bean Street in Richmond. A brick building, it was built in 1901 to replace a previous church, located further south on the same street, which had been destroyed by fire in 1900. Previous to the church union that resulted in the formation of the United Church of Canada, it was known as the Richmond Methodist Church, but afterwards, the church was named St. Paul's United Church.

St. Paul's United Church in Richmond.

St. Philip's Roman Catholic Church, Richmond

The history of St. Philip's Roman Catholic Parish goes back to 1818 when the village of Richmond was established. A wooden church was built in 1825. The 1830s to 1850s were turbulent times in Richmond with conflict between the Orange Order and the Irish Catholics. In 1857, St. Philip's was set ablaze, and the following year, a new stone church was built. Today, St. Philip's is the oldest parish within the Archdiocese of Ottawa and it will celebrate its 200th anniversary in the year 2019.

The history of St. Philip's Roman Catholic Church goes back to 1818.

Part Five

Churches of the
South-Eastern Ottawa Valley

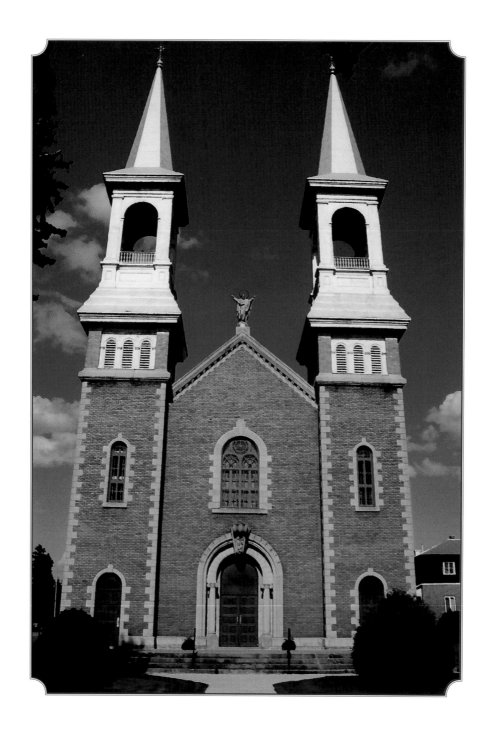

Sacre Coeur Roman Catholic Church, Bourget

This parish in which Sacre Coeur Roman Catholic Church is located was originally called The Brook, after a small river that crossed the Bear Brook, but the name was changed to Bourget in 1910. Between 1825 and 1863, many Francophones came to live in the area. In 1858, they built a chapel, which soon became too small. The second parish priest began the construction of a brick church, which was completed in 1889. Different renovations took place over the years. The old bell tower was replaced by two new ones, and a statue of the Sacred Heart was placed on the highest point on the roof. At the same time, two transepts were built. The old altars, the balustrades on the Lord's Table, the pulpit, and the Way of the Cross were replaced with impressive marble works of art. Stained glass windows were also added to beautify the church. This church has the distinction of having never fallen victim to fire.

The gold statue seems to be speaking to the visitor.

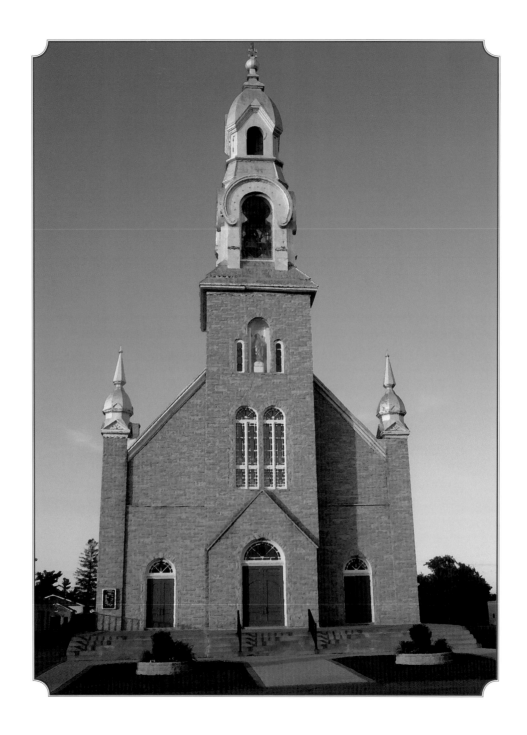

St. Euphemie Roman Catholic Church, Casselman

In 1844, Martin Casselman built a lumber mill at the foot of the Grand Chutes (Great Falls) on the Petite Nation (Little Nation River). Many people settled in the area and made a living from logging and farming. To accommodate the new community, Martin Casselman offered land for the construction of a church in 1876. A chapel was not built until 1885; then a parish priest had a church built in 1889.

In July 1891, a fire destroyed part of the town and much of the forest. Logging was no longer viable in the immediate area. Again on October 5, 1897, fire destroyed the entire town of Casselman as well as Limoges and Cheney. Two days later, parishioners decided to rebuild the church, which was blessed by Bishop Duhamel the following March even though the interior was not completed until 1907. In 1919, a third fire destroyed much of the parish. Rebuilding began right away.

St. Euphemie Parish celebrated its 120th anniversary in 2006. It is a credit to this congregation that its members have contended with disaster so many times and still survived together as a congregation. One reason may have been the leadership of Monseigneur Joseph Hercule Touchette. It is remarkable that Monseigneur Touchette's priesthood lasted sixty years; his time at St. Euphemie from 1897 to 1953 comprised fifty-six of them.

St. Euphemie stands as a result of the resilience of the congregation.

St. Luc Roman Catholic Church, Curran

Established in 1839, St. Luc Parish is the oldest parish in the eastern part of the diocese. Stone churches had been built in this parish in 1864 and 1876. Due to shifting ground, this latter church was replaced in 1895 by the current church and remains one of the most beautiful in the area.

St. Luc Parish is the oldest in the eastern part of the diocese.

St. Jacques Roman Catholic Church, Embrun

In 1845, the first settlers came to the Embrun area east of Ottawa. The first missionaries arrived around 1852, and the first chapel was built at the request of Bishop Guigues in 1856. In 1861, a new chapel replaced the old one, which had become too small. In 1880, a new place of worship was built on what was later revealed to be unstable ground. As a result, a replacement church had to be built. The site was blessed in 1891. The interior of the church was finally completed in 1906, and a steam heating system was installed in 1908. Cement steps and a carillon of five bells were added in 1910. It must be mentioned that at the turn of the century Embrun was one of the largest parishes in the diocese. Today, St. Jacques is one of the most beautiful churches in Eastern Ontario.

St. Jacques Roman Catholic Church is one of the most beautiful churches in Eastern Ontario.

St. Bernard Roman Catholic Church, Fournier

St. Bernard Parish was formed in 1867, the same year as the Canadian Confederation. As early as 1855, Bishop Guigues had blessed the site of a future church. Bernard Lemieux donated the land, and in 1859 a chapel was built and blessed, then given the name Bernard in honour of the benefactor, Bernard Lemieux.

During a visit in 1873, Bishop Guigues noted that the chapel was in a poor state of repair and requested that a new church be built. Construction of the new building did not take place until over a decade later. Finally work began in 1885. In 1886, the new stone church was blessed and opened for worship, but the interior was not completed until 1896.

In 1904, a carillon was added, and in 1918, beautiful stained glass windows were put in place. Coming across this church in the country during a Sunday drive through Eastern Ontario was a very pleasant surprise.

Finding St. Bernard Roman Catholic Church on a Sunday drive was a very pleasant surprise.

St. Viateur Roman Catholic Church, Limoges

The first chapel to serve the St. Viateur Parish was built in 1884 and enlarged in 1893. In 1897, fire destroyed the town and the chapel, but the church was rebuilt and blessed in 1898. Again in 1924, the church and the rectory fell victim to flames. The church was rebuilt with red brick and was blessed in 1925, again showing the perseverance of the congregation in light of the disastrous fires.

A church built by the perseverance of the congregation.

St. Andrew's Presbyterian Church, Spencerville

St. Andrew's Presbyterian Church will celebrate 177 years of Presbyterianism in Spencerville in 2012. The first Presbyterian church in the town was built in 1835, followed by a second new church in 1837. The cornerstone of the present beautiful, stone St. Andrew's Presbyterian Church was laid in 1877. When church members voted to join church union in 1925 (forming the United Church of Canada) the congregation was divided, but those who retained their affiliation with the Presbyterian Church have maintained a vigorous congregation to this day.

St. Andrew's Presbyterian Church, Spencerville.

St. Laurence O'Toole Roman Catholic Church, Spencerville

Located in the rural community of Spencerville, south of Ottawa, St. Laurence O'Toole Roman Catholic Church stands out as a lovely example of the many stone churches found in the area, and another of the churches where the ramparts are visible.

The cornerstone of St. Laurence O'Toole Church was laid on August 19, 1883, and the finished church was dedicated in September 1886. The church was dedicated to St. Laurence O'Toole (1128–1180), who was the Archbishop of Dublin, Ireland, in 1161.

Notice the very visible ramparts of St. Laurence O'Toole Roman Catholic Church.

Spencerville United Church, Spencerville

Spencerville United Church is a classically beautiful church situated in the historic village of Spencerville. As noted by Elva Richards McGaughey in *A Profile of Spencerville United Church*, "Spencerville, by 1850, was a village of some two hundred and fifty inhabitants. For these people, whatever their denomination, the church was a centre of religious and social life."

Spencerville United had its beginnings in the early Wesleyan Methodist Church. Elva McGaughey records that "[t]he most reliable record of Wesleyan Methodism in the Spencerville area is the Spencerville Circuit Book whose record begins in June 1862 and extends until 1924. . . . Building on the site of the present church, was started in the spring of 1871, and the building was dedicated January 8, 1873."

The original church was replaced by the present church shortly after the formation of the United Church of Canada in 1925, when Spencerville area Methodists and Presbyterians interested in church union decided they needed a new building. The new church was built at the present location in 1930. It was the start of the Depression years and times were tough; but the church, despite its heavy debt, maintained a shaky solvency throughout the 1930s. The 1940s brought better times. The mortgage, taken out years before, was paid off in 1947, and a mortgage-burning ceremony was held.

It is of particular interest that one of the key figures leading up to church union in 1925 was Dr. Rev. S. Dwight Chown, a minister at the Spencerville Methodist Church from 1887 to 1890. Dr. Chown had become the General Superintendent of the Canadian Methodist Church and was presiding in that role at the time of United Church union. Elva McGaughey observes that "Dr. Chown's important role in the founding of the United Church was commemorated by a stamp issued in 1975."

The present church, built of red brick and grey limestone, remains as one of three centres of religious activity in Spencerville.

The Spencerville United Church located in the centre of Spencerville.

Church Addresses

PART ONE
Churches of Ottawa within View of the Parliament Buildings

All Saints Anglican Church, 347 Richmond Road, Ottawa, Ontario K2A 0E7

All Saints Sandy Hill Anglican Church, 317 Chapel Street, Ottawa, Ontario K1N 7Z2

Blessed Sacrament Roman Catholic Church, 194 Fourth Avenue, Ottawa, Ontario K1S 2L3

Christ Church Cathedral, 439 Queen Street, Ottawa, Ontario K1R 5A6

Church of St. Mathias Anglican, 555 Parkdale Avenue, Ottawa, Ontario K1Y 1H9

Dominion Chalmers United Church, 355 Cooper Street, Ottawa, Ontario K2P 0G8

Eglise Unis St. Marc, 142 Lewis Street, Ottawa, Ontario K2P 0S7

Erskine Presbyterian Church, 343 Bronson Avenue, Ottawa, Ontario K1R 6G2

First Baptist Church, 140 Laurier Avenue West, Ottawa, Ontario K1P 5J4

First United Church, 397 Kent Street, Ottawa, Ontario K2P 2B1

Glebe-St. James United Church, 650 Lyon Street South, Ottawa, Ontario K1S 3Z7

Knox Presbyterian Church, 120 Lisgar Street, Ottawa, Ontario K2P 0C2

MacKay United Church, 39 Dufferin Road, Ottawa, Ontario K1M 2H3

Merivale United Church, 1876 Merivale Road, Nepean, Ontario K2G 1E6

Notre Dame Cathedral, 56 Guigues Avenue, Ottawa, Ontario K1N 5H5

Notre-Dame-de-Lourdes-de-Cyrville, 1187 Michael Street, Ottawa, Ontario K1J 7T2

Our Lady of the Visitation Roman Catholic Church, 5338 Bank Street, Gloucester, Ontario K1H 1X1

Southminster United Church, 15 Aylmer Avenue, Ottawa, Ontario K1S 3X1

St. Alban the Martyr Anglican Church, 454 King Edward Avenue, Ottawa, Ontario K1N 7M8

St. Andrew's Presbyterian Church, 82 Kent Street, Ottawa, Ontario K1P 5N9

Ste. Anne's Roman Catholic Church, 528 Old St. Patrick's Street, Ottawa, Ontario K1N 5L5

St. Anthony's Roman Catholic Church, 427 Booth Street, Ottawa, Ontario K1R 7K8

St. Bartholomew Anglican Church, 125 MacKay Street, Ottawa, Ontario K1M 2B4

St. Brigid's Roman Catholic Church, 310 St. Patrick's Street, Ottawa, Ontario K1N 5K5

St. Charles Roman Catholic Church, 135 Barrette Street, Vanier, Ontario K1L 7Z9

St. Francois d'Assise Roman Catholic Church, 20 Fairmont Street, Ottawa, Ontario K1Y 2K2

St. George's Roman Catholic Church, 415 Piccadilly Avenue, Ottawa, Ontario K1Y 0H3

St. Jean Baptiste Church (Eglise St-Jean-Baptiste), 96 Empress Avenue, Ottawa, Ontario K1R 7G3

St. John the Baptist Ukrainian Catholic Shrine, 952 Green Valley Crescent, Ottawa, Ontario K2C 3K7

St. Joseph's Roman Catholic Church, 151 Laurier Avenue East, Ottawa, Ontario K1N 6N8

St. Mary's Roman Catholic Church, 100 Young Street, Ottawa, Ontario K1Y 3P7

St. Matthew's Anglican Church, 217 First Avenue, Ottawa, Ontario K1S 2G5

St. Patrick's Basilica, 281 Nepean Street, Ottawa, Ontario K1R 5G2

St. Paul's-Eastern United Church, 473 Cumberland Street, Ottawa, Ontario K1N 7K1

St. Paul's Lutheran Church, 210 Wilborn Street, Ottawa, Ontario K1N 6L5

St. Peter's Lutheran Church, 400 Sparks Street, Ottawa, Ontario K1R 5A2

St. Theresa Roman Catholic Church, 95 Somerset Street West, Ottawa, Ontario K2P 0H3

PART TWO
Churches of Fitzroy, Goulbourn, Huntley, Torbolton, and March Townships in Ottawa West

St. John's Anglican Church, 3751 Kinburn Side Road, Antrim, Ontario K0A 2H0

Christ Church Anglican, 8944 Flewellyn Road, R.R. 3, Ashton, Ontario K0A 1B0

Melville Presbyterian Church, 8953 Flewellyn Road, R.R. 3, Ashton, Ontario K0A 1B0

Bells Corners United Church, 3955 Old Richmond Road, Nepean, Ontario K2H 5C5

St. James the Apostle Anglican Church, 3774 Carp Road, Carp, Ontario K0A 1L0

St. Michael's Roman Catholic Church, 1560 Corkery Road, R.R. 2, Carp, Ontario K0A 1LO

St. Paul's Anglican Church, 1118 Thomas Dolan Parkway, Dunrobin, Ontario K0A 1T0

Fallowfield United Church, 119 Steeple Hill Crescent, Fallowfield, Ontario K2R 1G1

St. Patrick's Roman Catholic Church, 15 Steeple Hill Crescent, Fallowfield, Ontario K2R 1G2

St. Andrew's United Church, 184 Carleton Street, Fitzroy Harbour, Ontario K0A 1X0

St. George's Anglican Church, 176 Shirrif Street, Fitzroy Harbour, Ontario K0A 1X0

St. Michael's Roman Catholic Church, 166 Kedey Street, Fitzroy Harbour, Ontario K0A 1X0

St. John's Anglican Church, 325 Sandhill Drive, Kanata, Ontario K2K 1X7

Christ Church Anglican, 3008 Carp Road, Carp, Ontario K0A 1L0

St. Isidore Roman Catholic Church, 1135 March Road, Kanata, Ontario K2K 1X7

St. Mary's Anglican Church, 2574 6th Line Road, North March, Ontario K0A 1T0

St. Thomas Anglican Church, 1619 Stittsville Main Street, Stittsville, Ontario K2S 1N5

Stittsville United Church, 6255 Fernbank Road, Stittsville, Ontario K2S 1X5

St. Thomas Anglican Church, 3794 Woodkilton Road, Woodlawn, Ontario K0A 3M0

PART THREE
Churches of the Madawaska and Mississippi River Valleys

Almonte United Church, 106 Elgin Street, Almonte, Ontario K0A 1A0

Auld Kirk, Concession 8, Almonte, Ontario K0A 1A0

Holy Name of Mary Roman Catholic Church, 134 Bridge Street, Almonte, Ontario K0A 1A0

Reformed Presbyterian Church, 273 Almonte Street, Almonte, Ontario K0A 1A0

St. John's Presbyterian Church, 111 Church Street, Almonte, Ontario K0A 1A0

St. Paul's Anglican Church, 70 Clyde Street, Almonte, Ontario K0A 1A0

Grace St. Andrew's United Church, 269 John Street North, Arnprior, Ontario K7S 2P3

St. John Chrysostom Roman Catholic Church, 295 Albert Street, Arnprior, Ontario K7S 2M7

St. Andrew's United Church, 1673 Burnstown Road, Burnstown, Ontario K7V 3Z4

St. Andrew's Presbyterian Church, 39 Bridge Street, Carleton Place, Ontario K7C 3P5

St. James Anglican Church, 225 Edmund Street, Carleton Place, Ontario K7C 3E7

Zion-Memorial United Church, 37 Franklin Street, Carleton Place, Ontario K7C 1R6

St. John's Anglican Church, Hwy 7 Innisville, Ontario K7H 3N3

St. Andrew's United Church, 115 Clarence Street, Lanark, Ontario K0G 1K0

St. Paul's Anglican Church, 2985 County Road 511, Lanark, Ontario K0G 1K0

St. Andrew's United Church, 2585 County Road 29, Pakenham, Ontario K0A 2X0

St. Peter Celestine Roman Catholic Church, 139 Renfrew Street, Pakenham, Ontario K0A 2X0

PART FOUR
Churches of the Rideau Valley

Christ Church Anglican, County Rd #2, 4419 Donnelly Drive, Burrett's Rapids, Ontario K0G 1B0

St. James Anglican Church, 128 Church Street, Franktown, Ontario K7A 4S7

St. Paul's United Church, Crampton Road, Franktown, Ontario K7C 3P1 (Mailing address: R.R. 6, 9603 Highway 15, Smiths Falls, Ontario K7A 4S7)

Trinity United Church, 6656 Rideau Valley Drive South, Kars, Ontario K0A 2E0

St. Brigid's Roman Catholic Mission, 2015 River Road, Manotick, Ontario K4M 1B0

St. James the Apostle Anglican Church, 1138 Bridge Street, Manotick, Ontario, K4M 1A3

Munster United Church, 2881 Munster Road, Munster Hamlet, Ontario K0A 3P0

Holy Trinity Anglican Church, 2372 Church Street, North Gower, Ontario K0A 2T0

North Gower United Church, 2332 Church Street, North Gower, Ontario K0A 2T0

St. John the Evangelist Roman Catholic Church, 2546 Stagecoach Road, Osgoode, Ontario K0A 2W0

St. John the Evangelist Anglican Church, 103 Maplewood Avenue, Oxford Mills, Ontario K0G 1S0

St. Andrew's Presbyterian Church, 1 Drummond Street West, Perth, Ontario K7H 3E3

St. James Anglican Church, 12 Harvey Street, Perth, Ontario K7H 1W4

St. John the Baptist Roman Catholic Church, 38 Wilson Street East, Perth, Ontario K7H 1L6

St. Paul's United Church, 25 Gore Street West, Perth, Ontario K7H 2L9

Prospect United Church, 414 Franktown Road, Prospect, Ontario K0A 1B0

St. Augustine's Anglican Church, 261 Franktown Road, Prospect, Ontario K0A 1B0

St. Andrew's Presbyterian Church, 3529 McBean Street, Richmond, Ontario K0A 2Z0

St. John's Anglican Church, 67 Fowler Street, Richmond, Ontario K0A 2Z0

St. Paul's United Church, 3452 McBean Street, Richmond, Ontario K0A 2Z0

St. Philip's Roman Catholic Church, 127 Burke Street, Richmond, Ontario K0A 2Z0

PART FIVE
Churches of the South-Eastern Ottawa Valley

Sacre Coeur Roman Catholic Church, 3756 Champlain Street, Bourget, Ontario K0A 1E0

St. Euphemie Roman Catholic Church, 726 Principale Street, Casselman, Ontario K0A 1M0

St. Luc Roman Catholic Church, Curran, Ontario K0B 1C0

St. Jacques Roman Catholic Church, 1041 Notre Dame, Embrun, Ontario K0A 1W0

St. Bernard Roman Catholic Church, 5142 County Road #10, Fournier, Ontario K0B 1G0

St. Viateur Roman Catholic Church, 154 Mabel Street, Limoges, Ontario K0A 2M0

St. Andrew's Presbyterian Church, 48 Bennett Street, Spencerville, Ontario K0E 1X0

St. Laurence O'Toole Roman Catholic Church, 48 Centre Street, Spencerville, Ontario K0E 1X0

Spencerville United Church, 16 Centre Street, Spencerville, Ontario K0E 1X0

Sources

Adam, Mohammed. "Crisis of Faith." *Ottawa Citizen*, October 11, 2009.

Botteriell, Barbara. *Stittsville: A Sense of Place.* Our World Publications, 1998.

Brown, Howard Morton. *Founded Upon a Rock; Carleton Place Recollections.* Juniper Books, 1984.

——. "St. James Church Franktown Oldest in the Valley." *Carleton Place Canadian*, January 26,1961.

Cook, Mary. "Valley Tales: St. Peter Celestine." *Forever Young (Ottawa Carleton Edition)*, June 2000.

Corbett, Ron. "Life in the City — A Downtown without Churches." *Ottawa Citizen*, February 17, 2007.

Daly, Michael. *Our Lady of the Visitation 140th Anniversary Commemorative Booklet 1845–1985*, 1985.

Dare, Patrick. "St. Isidore's Dreads Heritage Designation." *Ottawa Citizen*, May 5, 2009.

Edwards, Margaret Bunel, Edith Taylor Ashton and John Alexander Edmison. *Highlights from MacKay's History: MacKay United Church, 1975-1975.* Ottawa, ON: LoMor Printers Ltd., 1975.

Egan, Kelly. "From Log to Stone to Heated Floors." *Ottawa Citizen*, December 11, 2011.

Farr, David. *Completing the First Century 1898–1998: A Commemoration of Worship and Service in the Glebe.* St. Matthew's Anglican Church, Ottawa, 1998.

Fitzpatrick, Meagan. "The Legend of the Lilac." *Ottawa Citizen*, August 29, 2003.

Frith, Rowley. *First Baptist Church: Ottawa 1857–1957.* Published by the Advisory Committee of the Church for the Centenary Celebrations, 1957.

Goulbourn Historical Society and Museum. Various historical documents, Goulbourn Township, Stittsville, ON.

Goulbourn Township Historical Society. *Goulbourn Memories.* Goulbourn Township Historical Society, 1996.

Graham, John, and John Farley. *Tour of Nepean.* Nepean Local Architectural Conservation Society Advisory Committee Brochure, 1983.

Harvey, Bob. "Ashton's Christ Church an Enduring Monument to Its 160-Year History." *Ottawa Citizen*, January 9, 2005.

Harvey, Bob. "Basilica Can't Afford Much Needed Repairs." *Ottawa Citizen*, April 14, 2002.

Hendry, Shirley. *A History of St. John's Anglican Church, South March 1839–1989.* St. John's Anglican Church,1989.

Hurtubise, Pierre, Mark G. McGowan, and Pierre Savard. *Planted by Flowering Water: The Diocese of Ottawa, 1847–1997.* Ottawa, ON: University of St. Paul Novalis Publishing, 1998.

Lanark County Archives, Concession 7 Drummond Centre, Perth, ON.

Lockwood, Glenn J "A Cathedral in a City of Sawmills" in *Ex Cathedra: Newsletter of Christ Church Cathedral, Ottawa,* (April 2007), pp. 6-7 received from Dr. Lockwood.

Lofaro, Tony. "Wedding Was the Place to Be." *Ottawa Citizen*, February 11, 1999.

McGaughey, Elva R. *A Profile of Spencerville United Church.* Spencerville United Church, 1975.

McGill, Jean S. *A Pioneer History of the County of Lanark: Pioneer Churches and Ministers.* Dewdley, ON: Clay Publishing, 1979.

Morrison, Lloyd C. *A Month of Sundays: A Visit to Seventy Churches in the Ottawa Valley.* Burnstown, ON: General Store Publishing House, 1998.

Nankivell, Neville. "A Short History of St. Matthews, the Anglican Church in the Glebe." Adapted from the book, *A Church in the Glebe,* written by David Farr. St. Matthews Anglican Church, 1988.

Nyenhuis, Michael, Editor. *A Faith Journey — Photo History of the Ottawa Presbytery of the United Church of Canada, December 2004.* Carleton Place, ON: Ferguson Graphics, 2004.

Ottawa Journal, December 1930.

Our History 1888–1988. Parish Directory/History of the Church of St. Matthias, March 1988.

Renton, Audrey. *History of Trinity United Church, Kars, Ontario*. The Church, 1975.

Scribes Committee. *Sixty Years at Southminster United Church, Ottawa, Ontario 1932–1992*. Southminster United Church, 1992.

St. Andrew's Presbyterian Church Visitor's Guide. Ottawa, ON: July 1998.

Warburton, Wendy. "Church Gets New Lease on Life as Law Office." *Ottawa Citizen*, November 19, 1979.

Internet Websites

All Saints Anglican Church, Westboro. "The Beginning." On-line. ***http://www.allsaintswestboro.com/history.html*** (accessed January 2012).

The Anglican Parish of March. "History of the Parish of March." On-line. ***http://www.parishofmarch.ca/?q = who-we-are/parish-history*** (accessed January 2009 and June 2012).

Bells Corners United Church, Bells Corners. "Our History." On-line. http://***www.bcuc.org***/history.htm (accessed January 2010).

Blessed Sacrament Roman Catholic Church, The Glebe. Grace, John. "A History of Blessed Sacrament." *The Spirit of Blessed Sacrament*. On-line. http://***www.blessedsacrament.ca***/?page_id=6 (accessed January 2011).

Carleton Place Local History. On-line. http://***www.carletonplacelocalhistory.wordpress.com/category/churches/*** (accessed January 2012).

Christ Church Anglican, Carp Road. Thompson, Suzanne. "Early History of Christ Church, Parish of Huntley." *The Anglican Parish of Huntley, Christ Church Anglican, Carp Road*. On-line. http://***www.huntleyparish.com***/Parish_of_Huntley/C_C_Hist.html (accessed October 2010).

Christ Church Cathedral, Ottawa. "The Cathedral in Ottawa: History." On-line. http://www.ottawa.anglican.ca/cathedral/The_Cathedral.html#history (accessed October 2010).

Church of St. Matthias Anglican, Ottawa. "St. Matthias Church - A Brief History." On-line. http://www.stmatthias.ca/about-us/history/17-history-of-st-matthias.html (accessed August 2012).

Dominion-Chalmers United Church, Ottawa. "History of Dominion-Chalmers United Church Vignettes." On-line. http://www.dc-church.org/index.php?page=Vignettes (accessed April 2012).

Fallowfield United Church. "Our Church Heritage." *Fallowfield United Church 1886 to the Present*. On-line. http://***www.geocities.com/merivaleuc/fallowfield.html*** (accessed October 2010).

First Baptist Church, Ottawa. "History." On-line. http:// ***www.firstbaptistottawa.ca*** (accessed October 2009).

First United Church, Ottawa. "History." On-line. http://***www.firstunitedchurchottawa.org//index.php***?option=com_content&task=view&id=15&Itemid=67 (accessed January 2012).

Knox Presbyterian Church, Ottawa. "History." On-line. http://***www.knoxottawa.ca***/history/ (accessed February 2012).

Our Lady of the Visitation Roman Catholic Church, South Gloucester. Daley, Michael. "Historical Sketch of Our Lady of the Visitation." *Our Lady of the Visitation Church (South Gloucester, Ontario)*. On-line. ***http://www.olvis.ca/history.html*** (accessed August 2012).

St. Alban the Martyr Church, Ottawa. "St. Alban's Church." On-line. ***http://www.stalbanschurch.ca/index.php/who-we-are/st-albans*** (accessed November 2011).

St. Andrew's Presbyterian Church, Kent St., Ottawa. "The Building." On-line. http://***www.standrewsottawa.ca***/who-we-are/the-building (accessed December 2011).

St. Andrew's Presbyterian Church, Perth. "A History of St. Andrew's Presbyterian Church, Perth, Ontario." On-line. http//***www.standrewsperth.com***/ (accessed October 2010).

St. Bartholomew Anglican Church, Ottawa. "The History and Architecture of St. Barts." On-line. ***http://www.stbartsottawa.ca***/history_part1.html (accessed January 2012).

St. George's Anglican Church, Fitzroy Harbour. "The History of St. George's Anglican Church." On-line. http://***www.anglicanfitzroyparish.com/history_stgeorge.htm*** (accessed January 2012).

St. George's Catholic Church, Ottawa. "The History of St. George's Catholic Church." On-line. *http://www.saintgeorges.ca/*?page_id=38 (accessed March 2012).

St. James the Apostle Anglican Church, Carp. Rivington, Helen. "Early History of St. James Church, Parish of Huntley." *St. James Church, Parish of Huntley.* On-line. http//.www.huntleyparish.com/Parish_of_Huntley/St_J_Hist.html (Accessed October 2011).

St. James the Apostle Anglican Church, Manotick. "History." On-line. http://*www.manotick.org/stjames*-manotick.org/history/ (accessed February 2012).

St. James the Apostle Anglican Church, Perth. "About the Parish." On-line. http//*www.superaje.com/~stjamesperth/*st.james_perth/WELCOME.html (accessed October 2010).

St. James United Church, Ottawa. "History." *Glebe* On-line. http://www.glebestjames.com/?page_id=18 (accessed October 2011).

St. John's Anglican Church, Antrim. Archeion Ontario's Archival Information Network. "St. John's Anglican Church (Antrim, Ont.)." On-line. http://*www.archeion.ca/st-johns*-church-anglican-antrim-ontario-fonds;rad (accessed October 2011).

St. John the Baptist Anglican Church, Richmond. "Brief History." On-line. http://*www.saintjohnsrichmond.ca/* (accessed October 2010).

St. John the Baptist Ukrainian Catholic Shrine, Ottawa. "Our History." On-line. http://*www.st-john-baptist-shrine.ca/history.htm* (accessed January 2012).

St. Joseph's Parish. "History." On-line. http://www.st-josephs.ca/about/history (accessed October 2011).

St. Mary's Roman Catholic Church, Civic Hospital. Connolly, Greg. "New St. Mary's Church Completed." *Ottawa Citizen*, June 20, 1951. *St. Mary's Parish Roman Catholic Church.* On-line. http://*www.stmarysottawa.ca* (accessed January 2012).

St. Patrick's Basilica, Ottawa. "History." On-line. http://*www.basilica.org/pages/enduring_faith.php* (accessed January 2010).

St. Patrick's Catholic Church, Fallowfield. "Brief History of Parish." On-line. http://*www.stpatricks.nepean.on.ca/directory/pg3.html* (accessed November 2011).

St. Paul's-Eastern United Church. "A Brief History of St. Paul's-Eastern United Church." On-line. http://*www.stpaulseastern.com/*?p=11&t=Our-History (accessed November 2011).

St. Paul's United Church, Franktown. Kidd, Faith. (1995). "The History of St. Paul's United Church, Franktown 1816–1895." *Boyd's Franktown Pastoral Charge.* On-line. *http://www.refrewpresbytery.org/boyds-franktown/franktown/stpauls%20history.html* (accessed February 2012).

St. Paul's United Church, Perth. "Church History." On-line. http://*www.stpauls-uc-perth.org/* (accessed February 2012).

St. Paul's United Church, Perth. "The History of St. Paul's United Church, Perth." *Welcome to the Perth and Area Christian Website.* On-line. http://*www.perthareachurches.ca* (accessed February 2012).

St. Peter Celestine Roman Catholic Church, Pakenham. "St. Peter Celestine Church." On-line. http://*www.stpetercelestine.ca/html/virtual_tour.html* (accessed November 2011).

St. Peter's Evangelical Lutheran Church, Ottawa. "History." On-line. *http://www.stpetersottawa.ca*/about-our-church/history/ (accessed January 2010).

St. Thomas Anglican Church, Woodlawn. Botteriell, Barbara. (n.d.) "A History of the Anglican Parish of St. Thomas." *St. Thomas Anglican Church.* On-line. *http://www.magma.ca/~stthoms/history.htm*l (accessed February 2012).

St. Thomas Anglican Church, Woodlawn. "The History of St. Thomas Anglican Church." On-line. http://*www.anglicanfitzroyparish.com/history_stthomas.htm* (accessed January 2012).

Stittsville United Church. "Our History." On-line. http://*www.suchurch.com/*about/hist.html (accessed January 2012).

Zion-Memorial United Church. "History of Zion-Memorial United Church Relating to the Methodist Congregation" and "History of Zion-Memorial United Church Relating to the St. Andrew's Presbyterian Congregation." *Welcome to Zion-Memorial United Church.* On-line. http://*www.zion-memorial.ca/history.htm* (accessed January 2012).

About the Author

Alan H. Bentley was born and raised in Nova Scotia. While growing up on an apple and poultry farm in the Annapolis Valley, he attended the Berwick Baptist Church with his parents and his grandfather, who were faithful attendees. Following high school, he attended the Nova Scotia Agricultural College, the Ontario Agricultural College, and the University of Guelph. Alan located to Ottawa in 1967, where he had a career with Agriculture Canada before retiring in 1995. It was at this time that he developed an interest in the churches of Ottawa. As a result, he roamed the area for the past fifteen years, photographing most of the churches on the Ontario side of the Ottawa River. It is this interest that has resulted in the publication of this book.

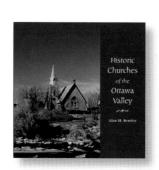

GSPH

TO ORDER MORE COPIES:
General Store Publishing House
499 O'Brien Road, Box 415, Renfrew, Ontario, Canada K7V 4A6
Tel 1.800.465.6072 • Fax 1.613.432.7184
www.gsph.com